The Legal Environment of Translation

Translation is subject to a complex and unique set of legal rules that govern its various practical and intellectual aspects. These rules derive from very different legal areas, such as intellectual property and labour law. While useful from a strictly legal point of view, the heterogeneity of sources operates as a major hurdle in terms of understanding the overall legal framework within which translation operates.

This book offers a general overview of the legal rules applicable to different aspects of translation, allowing translators and other interested parties to form a broad and coherent picture of the rules applicable in this area. It draws on the provisions of the main legal systems of the world, as well as the basic international agreements relevant in this area, thus offering both a comparative perspective of the legal issues involved and a guide to relevant national legal rules. In addition to a description and analysis of the legal issues and rules involved, the book also presents hypothetical cases, with a discussion of the problems they pose and possible solutions. It explains the theoretical structure of the rules under discussion as well as their practical implications.

The language and methodology of the book are sufficiently accessible to allow lawyers, translators and those who require translation work but do not have a formal legal background to follow the arguments presented.

Guillermo Cabanellas is a Professor at the National University of Buenos Aires and a Visiting Professor at the University of Illinois. He is a member of the editorial board of the *World Intellectual Property Organization Journal* and former research fellow at the Max Planck Institute, Munich. He is the author of more than forty books, including several bilingual and monolingual legal dictionaries, and over one hundred legal articles published in different countries.

The Legal Environment of Translation

Guillermo Cabanellas

Taylor & Francis Group

LONDON AND NEW YORK

First published 2014
by Routledge
2 Park Square, Milton Park, Abingdon, Oxon OX14 4RN

and by Routledge
711 Third Avenue, New York, NY 10017

Routledge is an imprint of the Taylor & Francis Group, an informa business

© 2014 Guillermo Cabanellas

The right of Guillermo Cabanellas to be identified as author of this work has been asserted in accordance with sections 77 and 78 of the Copyright, Designs and Patents Act 1988.

All rights reserved. No part of this book may be reprinted or reproduced or utilised in any form or by any electronic, mechanical, or other means, now known or hereafter invented, including photocopying and recording, or in any information storage or retrieval system, without permission in writing from the publishers.

Trademark notice: Product or corporate names may be trademarks or registered trademarks, and are used only for identification and explanation without intent to infringe.

British Library Cataloguing in Publication Data
A catalogue record for this book is available from the British Library

Library of Congress Cataloging in Publication Data
A catalog record for this title has been applied for

ISBN: 978-1-138-79080-3 (hbk)
ISBN: 978-1-138-79082-7 (pbk)
ISBN: 978-1-131-57639-8 (ebk)

Typeset in Times New Roman by
Delta Typesetters, Cairo, Egypt

CONTENTS

Preface		ix
1.	**The Legal Framework of Translation**	**1**
1.1	The practical importance of the legal framework of translation	1
1.2	A brief description of the world's legal systems	2
1.3	Determining the applicable law	5
1.4	Jurisdiction issues	7
1.5	Special regulations on translation	10
1.6	Translations in court	11
Case studies		12
2.	**Comparative and International Copyright Protection**	**14**
2.1	Copyright and its legal significance for translations	14
2.2	Copyright protection throughout the world	15
2.3	Protected works	18
2.4	Categories of protected works	21
2.5	Works excluded from protection	24
2.6	Special categories of works	25
2.7	Formal requirements	27
2.8	Ownership	28
2.9	Works created by several persons	30
2.10	Works made for hire	32
2.11	Assignments and licences	33
2.12	Exclusive rights	34
2.13	Economic or exploitation rights	35
2.14	Moral rights	38
2.15	Term of protection	39
2.16	Limitations on and exemptions from copyright protection	40
2.17	Infringement and remedies	43
2.18	Neighbouring rights	45
2.19	The international copyright protection system	46
Case studies		50
3.	**The Copyright Protection of Translations**	**52**
3.1	Basic rules of copyright protection as applied to translations	52
3.2	The legal concept of translation	53
3.3	The right of translation	58

3.4	Ownership of copyright in translations	62
3.5	The legal content of copyright in translation	67
3.6	Term of protection	70
3.7	Limitations on and exceptions from copyright in translation	70
3.8	Infringement of copyright in translations. Applicable remedies	72
3.9	Contracts related to copyright in translations	73
	Case studies	74

4. Protection of Translations by Confidentiality — 76

4.1	The functions of confidentiality in the area of translation	76
4.2	Terminology	77
4.3	Confidentiality protection throughout the world	78
4.4	The protection of confidential information by unfair competition law	81
4.5	The criminal law protection of confidential information	86
4.6	Contract law protection of confidential information	87
4.7	Protection of information under the rules on privacy	89
4.8	Liabilities for unjust enrichment in connection with the use of information	90
4.9	Tort liability as to conduct related to information	91
4.10	Labour law protection of information	92
4.11	Miscellaneous legal sources of protection of information	93
4.12	The effects of confidentiality obligations on translations	94
4.13	The protection of translation work by means of confidentiality	96
	Case studies	98

5. Labour Law Protection of Translations and Translators — 101

5.1	Labour law and its applicability to translations	101
5.2	The translator as employee	102
5.3	Intellectual property rights in translations produced by employees	106
5.4	Rights in confidential information in the context of employment relationships	109
5.5	Employer–employee competition	110
	Case studies	111

6. Contracts Related to Translation — 114

6.1	The contractual framework of translation	114

6.2	Negotiating and entering into an agreement	114
6.3	Agreements related to translation	117
6.4	Contractual provisions on payment for translation work	120
6.5	Copyright in the context of contracts related to translation	122
6.6	Breach of contract	124
6.7	Contract termination	126
6.8	Dispute resolution	128
Case studies		130

Bibliography 133

Index 135

Preface

Translation from a legal point of view

All human conduct may be examined from a legal point of view. It may be considered illegal, criminal, valid, void; it may be viewed as the source of additional legal relationships or as the exercise of a legal right. Translation is no exception to this general rule.

The legal analysis of translation is of special interest for several reasons. Translating is a complex activity, with distinctive features (Bellos 2011, Venuti 1995a) and as such it creates special legal issues. Generally, the legal aspects of translation have been examined from the point of view of copyright law (Venuti 1995b); however, as this study will show, there are several other legal dimensions to translation, related to the complexity and peculiarities of this activity. Thus, we are dealing with an area of the law defined not only by its content and users, but also by the specific issues it raises and the legal solutions that have been developed accordingly.

In addition, translation is a vast and permanently changing business. The value of translation work is enormous, from an economic as well as from other viewpoints, and this huge endeavour is possible only within the framework of specific legal rules. The investments made by translators – in terms of their work and of their training – and by the persons acquiring their services and products are only possible if such services and products are reasonably protected and not open to unauthorized use by persons who have not participated in the translation process or in its financing.

Finally, translation frequently takes place without stakeholders' adequate knowledge of its legal protection and implications. Much of the translation work taking place in the world has a low individual value, although it may be part of a business with a huge total turnover. Thus, it is not possible for the parties participating in this activity – as translators or as users of translations – to engage in lengthy negotiations about their contractual relationships, nor in legal investigations about the scope of their rights. Translation work frequently takes place with the understanding that a "reasonable" set of legal rules governs such work, but without detailed knowledge about the actual contents and meaning of such rules. In more technical terms, the characteristics of translation activities do not allow them to bear high transaction costs, as would result from protracted contractual negotiations or detailed legal research. Hence, translation work frequently takes place on the basis of mutual agreement about the basic aspects of such work, but with one or both parties not knowing the frequently complex legal implications of their agreement. This makes the analysis of such implications particularly important.

This book follows a comparative law perspective. It is not based on a specific national legal system, but rather on the common features of the different national laws. This is possible because there are common or similar solutions, applied by the different national legal systems, to the issues posed by translation. However, the possibilities of this type of analysis should not be exaggerated. There is no coherent world law, in this or other legal areas, but rather a complex system in which hundreds of independent national legal systems coexist with each other and with a rather vague and weak international law. If some uniformity transpires from this enormously complex legal structure, it is because the practical conflicts raised by translations are frequently the same in all the countries of the world, and also because in the area of the rules applicable to translation – particularly copyright – several international treaties have created a fairly detailed common framework, which is generally lacking in other legal areas. But real translation issues do not take place in the abstract dimension of comparative law, but rather in the context of concrete conflicts and relationships governed by specific national rules. Hence, the determination of the actual rules applicable to actual legal conflicts or relationships requires – in the field of translation as elsewhere – going beyond the general outline provided by comparative law. This in turn implies a dual process: determining the national law (or laws) applicable to a given set of facts, and defining the rules governing the case under such law.

Purpose of this book. Matters to be covered

The problems discussed in this book involve primarily translators and persons using their work. It seeks to provide a general overview of the legal rules applicable to these problems, taking into account the main legal systems of the world. It is not an exhaustive analysis of the rules applicable to translation under such legal systems, a work whose scope would greatly exceed the limits of this work.

In our experience, translation work is frequently undertaken and paid for without adequate knowledge of the legal problems such work poses nor of the possible solutions to such problems. Although, as in other areas of the law, the actual answer to concrete legal problems requires a detailed description of the different factual elements involved and of the national or other legal provisions applicable to such set of facts, it is possible to be aware of the main legal issues raised by translation work, and of the basic legal framework applicable to such issues, by means of the general principles applicable in the field. This possibility is strengthened by the fact that international treaties require, in the areas of copyright and intellectual property protection, compliance with certain minimum international standards. But the actual solution for real legal problems raised by translation will always require knowledge of the national rules applicable in each case.

No prior knowledge of copyright law or of any specific national legal system is required to follow the analysis included in this book. Familiarity with the issues and practices of translation is convenient but not necessary. The legal terminology employed is understandable by a non-specialist person fluent in the English language.

The legal analysis will begin, in Chapter 1, with a brief description of the world's legal systems; it is in the context of these different legal systems that the rules applicable to translations exist and are applied.

Copyright has been, traditionally, the principal legal instrument for the protection of translations. Given the importance of copyright protection in the context of the legal environment of translation, the elements of comparative and international copyright protection will be described in Chapter 2, followed in Chapter 3 by a description of the basic rules of copyright protection as applied to translations. Chapter 3 will also discuss other copyright issues of translation, such as the determination of what qualifies as a translation from a copyright perspective, the allocation of copyright on translations, the contents of such copyright, and the legal regime applicable to contracts related to the copyright protection of translations.

Translations may also be protected by means of confidentiality. This type of protection is governed by a complex and peculiar set of rules, to be examined in Chapter 4.

Chapter 5 will analyse the labour law protection of translations. A large proportion of translation work is undertaken in the context of employment relationships, and this context may significantly alter the rules applicable to the translation work as part of an employee's obligations.

Finally, Chapter 6 will discuss the characteristics and effects of contracts related to translations. This discussion reflects the fact that translations are frequently undertaken in a legal context previously defined by the translator and the user of the resulting translations. Such contracts pose multiple legal issues, some common to all types of contract, and some peculiar to translations.

Many countries have enacted special laws and regulations governing translation. These rules apply to matters such as the professional qualifications of translators, the requirements applicable to translations to be used for judicial or administrative purposes, and the remuneration of translators in general or in particular situations such as court work. These special regulatory systems will be described in Chapter 1, and their effects on other legal aspects of translation shall be examined in the following chapters in connection with the different issues on which such regulatory systems have a significant impact.

1. The Legal Framework of Translation

1.1 The practical importance of the legal framework of translation

As we noted in the Preface, most translation activity takes place without the parties involved having significant awareness of the legal framework in which they operate. This activity normally takes place according to the informal rules of the trade, regarding such matters as payment, responsibility for inaccuracies or delays and ownership of the translation. In the case of translations produced for publication, the legal framework tends to be more explicit, in the form of relatively simple contracts.

The underlying complexity of the legal relationships resulting from translations becomes evident in cases of conflict. These cases are relatively rare, in practice, but they bring forward multiple legal questions normally ignored by the parties involved in translation. For example:

– Who owns the translation in the absence of an agreement about such ownership?
– Is the translator liable for doing the translation of a work without proper authorization by the person owning the copyright in the work to be translated?
– Is the translator subject to confidentiality obligations in the absence of an express agreement to that effect?
– What payment is due to the translator in the absence of a previous agreement between the parties?
– To what use may the translation be put?
– May the person who ordered the translation revise it or change it?

The legal rules applicable to these questions have a significant impact on the long-term profitability of translation activities and on the way parties structure their contractual relationships in this field. Both the translators and the parties using their services will try to structure such relationships so as to avoid liabilities.

However, many of the legal aspects of translation refer to relationships with third parties, other than the translator and the commissioning agent. Both the translator and the person paying for the translation will normally be interested in protecting the translation from claims by third parties and from the unauthorized use of the translation. It is impossible to enter into contracts with all potential users of a translation, and the legal system has created a set of intellectual property rules which determine the rights of translators with regard to their works, even in the absence of any contractual relationship with the persons having access to translations.

A translation, once it has been produced, may be distributed and used throughout the world. Obviously, this potential worldwide distribution has significant implications for the value and effects of the translation. This raises a number of major legal questions whose answers bear on the way translation is undertaken, protected and paid for. It is necessary to determine to what extent translations are protected in the different countries of the world, even if they originate – in each case – in only one or a few of them. Also, in the case of a conflict about a given translation – e.g. about its ownership, use, payment, etc. – it must be determined which law or laws will govern such conflict, and which courts or tribunals will have jurisdiction over the case. If contracts are entered into in connection with a certain translation, questions will arise about which law governs these contracts, and to what extent they may be enforced in different jurisdictions.

1.2 A brief description of the world's legal systems

Multiple and diverse legal systems are applicable in the world. Hence, the rights and obligations relative to a given translation may be governed by one or more of these systems.

An initial description of these systems can identify so-called international law – sometimes also referred to as public international law – and the national legal systems of each of the states in which the world is divided. International law is the result of customs created by the conduct of states and of international agreements. It basically relates to states, in the sense that it creates rights and obligations in favour of or bearing on states. International law is highly significant in the area of translation, since several international agreements, to which most of the countries of the world are bound, provide certain minimum standards for intellectual property in general and for the protection of translations in particular.

The structure of international law is different, from several perspectives, from that of national legal systems. International law is not created by a central authority – a parliament, a legislature or other similar body – but rather by agreement between two or more states, or by repeated conduct having a customary character due to its acceptance as such by the international community. Multinational bodies, such as the United Nations, have very limited powers with regard to the creation of international law.

There are no central authorities in charge of the enforcement of international law. There are no courts with the power to enforce on states the contents of international law. The international courts that do exist – such as the International Court of Justice – cannot enforce their judgments, by means of public force, in the way in which a national court can proceed to such enforcement by means of the physical force at its disposal. International courts do have certain enforcement rights, but these must take place through the states which are part of the international community, or through international mechanisms which finally rely on the enforcement means provided by national states. In addition, the international courts that do exist have jurisdiction in very specific domains, and do not have jurisdiction regarding conflicts involving international law in general. Thus, decisions on international law conflicts are to a large extent left to the whims of the individual states which are subject to the obligations created by such law, and enforcement of whatever position is taken in that respect will depend on the effective power of each state. Under these circumstances, it is arguable whether international law is law at all; it certainly works very differently than national legal systems. Its effects, however, can be very significant. In particular, in the area of intellectual property law, it is impossible to understand such law outside of the context created by international law. The contemporary national intellectual property law systems are to a large extent the consequence of international agreements; the enforcement of such agreements may be relatively weak, but they have nevertheless shaped intellectual property laws, throughout the world, in accordance with their provisions.

Each national state has its own legal system. The structure and characteristics of these systems are highly variable. Some are organized on the basis of a written constitution – e.g. the United States – some have constitutional systems not resulting from a single written text – e.g. the United Kingdom – and some do not have an explicit constitutional framework. The relative position of statutory law, religious law, customs and case law varies greatly from one country to another. Also, some countries, such as Germany and Argentina, treat international law – or elements thereof – as part of their domestic legal systems, while other states – such as the United States – require international law to be formally accepted by internal law for it to be fully enforceable under their respective legal systems.

It is possible to classify national legal systems into several groups, based on the existence of common characteristics, legal concepts and traditions (see David and Brierley 1985; Reimann and Zimmermann 2008). Thus, for example, one may distinguish between civil law systems, Anglo-American legal systems, collectivistic legal systems, Muslim tradition legal systems, Chinese legal systems, etc. There is no single classification, and in fact these categories create relatively arbitrary groupings, which can be modified depending on the use being made of the relevant classification. Civil law systems are historically based on Roman law, but the legal systems of Germany and other northern European countries include, together with Roman law elements, rules, concepts and institutions derived from their own historical development. In fact, all legal systems include elements taken from different historical and cultural backgrounds.

There are several basic elements in each legal system which are used for purposes of including such systems in one of the groups into which the world's legal systems are normally classified. The first group of elements relates to the sources of the law, in other words what constitutes law in each legal system. Law may result from such sources as statutes, customs, court and administrative cases, regulations, generally accepted legal principles, or the opinions of legal writers or moral or religious authorities, etc. The various groups of legal systems place different emphasis on these sources. For example, civil law systems place more emphasis on statutory law, which theoretically is the basis of all these legal systems, and on the opinions of legal writers, which are frequently used by courts to "interpret" the statutory law; the Anglo-American legal system gives a broader role to case law, which is considered to be the source of many of its rules, and has developed complex technical instruments to apply, interpret and modify such case law. An example of this difference may be found in the copyright area. Civil law systems provide a detailed and exhaustive statutory list of exceptions to copyright protection, such as those applicable to political speeches or software back-up copies; American law has a broader authorization of "fair use", whose content is determined by a constantly evolving case law.

A second group of distinguishing elements consists of the legal concepts and terminology used by each system. This is not a matter of language, but rather of ideas. Concepts such as equity, laches, corporation or perpetuity have a technical sense under Anglo-American law which has no exact equivalent in other legal systems. Reciprocally, concepts such as juridical act, juridical fact or business association have a characteristic and central meaning in civil law systems, but are non-existent or irrelevant in other systems.

A third group of characteristics used to classify legal systems is based on the historical development of each national law. Civil law systems historically have been based on Roman law and on the civil codes enacted in continental Europe as from the beginning of the nineteenth century; Anglo-American legal systems are based on English common law; legal systems from the Muslim tradition are based on Islamic law, etc.

These classifications should not be used misleadingly when determining how actual national legal systems are created and operate. Contemporary Anglo-American systems have vast and complex statutory laws, though it should be pointed out that the technique used for drafting such laws is different from that used by civil law countries. Countries of the civil law tradition make extensive use of case law, although the techniques applied to determine the contents and limits of such law are somewhat different from those used in Anglo-American systems. Case law is generally based on the *stare decisis* principle, i.e. the idea that courts should apply their previous holdings as to the applicable law to new cases. But this principle is applied with various degrees of flexibility in each national legal system, and enforced through different mechanisms. English law is especially strict in its respect for precedents; under American law it is possible to "distinguish" new cases from old, and even to explicitly overrule precedents; under Argentine law, a decision inconsistent with previous case law may result in a special decision by all the members of several courts of appeal, unifying the applicable rules for the future; under French law appeals are heard at special courts, with jurisdiction in cases of inconsistency with previous case law.

Most countries, in fact, have built their national laws with elements taken from different cultural spheres. For example, Argentina, which is generally considered as part of the civil law tradition, has a constitutional system based – sometimes verbatim – on U.S. law, while its private law is clearly based on continental European precedents; Israeli law has elements that date back to the use of English law prior to independence, together with aspects drawn from civil law and from religious law; Japanese law includes rules copied from continental European and U.S. sources. Sometimes, the technique of "legal transplant" is used, pursuant to which parts of an alien legal system are introduced into a national law belonging to a different cultural group. In this manner, Japan "borrowed", during the nineteenth and twentieth centuries, laws or codes originating in Germany or the U.S., as part of a general modernization process of its legal system; Turkey "borrowed" the Swiss Code of Obligations, etc.

In addition, the division of national legal systems into "families" or cultural groupings is weakened by the increasing contemporary influence of international agreements and legal sources. For instance, the national laws of member countries of the European Union are increasingly shaped by the need to comply with the requirements set out by European Community law, such as those included in directives and regulations. In other cases, treaties with a potentially universal scope determine to a large extent the contents of national law; this is especially the case in intellectual property matters, such as copyright or patents. Although the individual countries still retain broad powers to shape their own laws, within the limits set by these treaties, these have contributed to a significant degree of homogeneity in intellectual property laws throughout the world.

1.3 Determining the applicable law

Suppose that X, a publisher operating in the United States, acquires the copyright on a book written by Y, an author living in Spain. X then contacts Z, a translator living in Mexico, to translate Y's work into English. The different aspects of this set of facts create multiple legal issues; there will be copyright in Y's book, copyright in the translation, a contract between X and Y, another contract between Y and Z, etc. Each of these aspects has contacts with or is located in different countries. In the case described above, copyright over Y's book has potential effects not only in Spain and the United States, but also in other countries of the world. X, upon acquiring such copyright, will be interested in knowing the extent of the protection it is acquiring in the different countries of the world, and not only in the United States or Spain. Similarly, if X and Z enter into an agreement on the translation of Y's work, both parties will wish to know what national contract law governs such agreement. The parties may include a choice-of-law provision, in which case they will have to determine to what extent such provision is valid and enforceable in other countries. Also, they may enter into the agreement without including a choice-of-law clause, and in that case they will be concerned with what the applicable law will be in case of a conflict related to that contract.

Since national laws give different solutions to a given case, determining what the law applicable to a case will be is an essential element to defining the rights of the parties involved in that case. This determination becomes increasingly important, in practice, due to the frequency of cases having relevant contacts with different countries.

The different national legal systems apply their own rules – called *conflict of laws rules* – to determine what law will be used to decide a case with international elements. There are no rules with global validity for this purpose, although some international agreements do include conflict of laws provisions with regard to specific issues. Therefore, in the case of a possible conflict or litigation with multinational elements, it is not possible to know what the applicable law will be until a determination is made about the court or authority that will decide the case. Once such court or authority is determined, it will apply its national conflict of laws rules to decide what national law or laws to apply to the case. Such conflict of laws rules may refer the case to a foreign law or require the use of the laws of the same country whose conflict of laws rules are being applied.

Even if the conflict of laws rules applied in a given case refer initially to the laws of a specific country, there may be additional obstacles to the use of such law by the court. The foreign law may be contrary to the court's public policy, i.e. the rules and principles which are an essential part of the court's legal system and that such legal system will not allow to be displaced. Courts will normally not apply or enforce foreign rules conflicting with such public policy. Also, the parties involved in the case may have structured their relationships so as to seek the enforcement of a law that would not normally be applicable to such relationships; conflict of laws rules may prevent the use of foreign laws resulting from what may be considered as a fraudulent arrangement aimed at avoiding the effects of the law normally applicable to the case.

In some cases, conflict of laws rules impose express limitations on the effects of foreign laws. For example, country X may not recognize a corporation organized under the laws of country Y if the main activity of such corporation is located in X.

In other cases, the local provisions applied by a court include special rules relative to legal relationships with foreign elements, instead of the court applying rules determining whether foreign or local rules will be applicable to a case. For example, if a foreign corporation wishes to operate in country Z, country Z will impose certain registration, domicile and representation requirements on such corporations, unilaterally determined by country Z's laws, regardless of what national law is applicable to the organization and other corporate matters related to that foreign corporation.

Different conflict of laws rules have been developed for the various types of issue that may arise in the context of cases with multinational elements.[1] In the case of contracts, the parties are generally free to choose the law applicable to their contractual relationships, provided such law has some reasonable contact with the issues raised by the relevant contract and that the chosen law does not infringe the public policy of the country whose courts have jurisdiction over an eventual case. In the absence of choice-of-law contractual clauses, each conflict of laws system includes rules to determine the laws applicable to contractual disputes. Some systems are based on specific characteristics of the relevant contract. For example, some legal systems will apply to a contract the law of the country where the domicile of the party performing the defining obligation of the agreement is located, while others focus on the location where the characteristic or main obligation resulting from the agreement is performed. These systems require additional rules determining what is meant by the "defining" or "characteristic obligation of the agreement". Other legal systems require the courts to examine the agreement as a whole, so as to determine the country with which the agreement has the closer contact, or to decide where the "centre of gravity" of the relevant legal relationship is located.

In international cases involving intellectual property, each country determines the scope of application of its laws – which generally is based on the territory of the country whose law is being applied – and the party claiming protection under one or more national laws will justify their applicability by invoking the violation of rights falling within the scope of protection of such national laws (see Fawcett and Torremans 1998). For instance, if a copyright owner considers that his or her copyright is being violated within France, that owner will claim ownership of copyright under French law, and French law will determine whether the claimed violation falls within the reach of French copyright.

1.4 Jurisdiction issues

The effectiveness of the rights related to translations depends on the existence of adequate legal remedies, to be sought before courts, administrative bodies or

---

[1] See, under U.S. law, Hay, Borchers and Symeonides (2010); under English law, Fawcett, Carruthers and North (2008).

arbitrators. Determining which courts, administrative bodies or arbitrators may have jurisdiction over a given case is an essential step for a person interested in assessing the real degree of protection such person's rights will receive. In many countries the rule of law is, to say the least, theoretical, and many of the statutory provisions theoretically in effect are not worth the paper they are printed on. This is especially the case with intellectual property rights. In many developing countries some of these rights are completely unenforceable in real life. For instance, most copies of films, music and software made and distributed in some of these countries are produced and sold in violation of the intellectual property rights held for these works, and either the courts will not recognize these rights or it will be impossible to enforce whatever decision the courts reach in a specific case.

There is no international system defining jurisdiction rules or assigning jurisdiction powers to each state. Whatever international courts or dispute resolution bodies exist – such as the International Court of Justice and the dispute resolution system of the World Trade Organization – have jurisdiction only with regard to very limited cases and persons. International intellectual property disputes brought before the World Trade Organization relate only to national states; a private person cannot bring a claim under this system.

With few exceptions – such as those derived from bilateral or multilateral treaties – each country determines unilaterally the scope of its jurisdiction. This implies that, with regard to a given case, one, several or no countries may unilaterally decide that they have jurisdiction. If only one national court or court system exercises jurisdiction over a given case, the possibilities of international judicial conflict are limited. But it may happen that several states claim jurisdiction over a given case, or that all the states involved decide not to exercise jurisdiction over a case. In these hypothetical situations, there is no supranational system leading to a coherent solution. If several courts of different states claim jurisdiction, they may enter into a judicial conflict situation, leading to contradictory results. If no court exercises jurisdiction, the plaintiff may find itself without legal protection. These results are in contrast with the solutions normally applied within a given legal system – particularly federal court systems, such as those of the U.S. and Brazil – in which the parties may appear before a higher court requesting a determination as to the lower court with jurisdiction over a case, if lower courts do not reach a coherent solution by themselves.

In cases having multinational elements, even a favourable decision issued by a national court may be useless for the party obtaining such decision. If a judgment is issued by a court from country A, ordering a person located in country B to pay a certain amount to the plaintiff, this judgment will be basically useless if the defendant has no assets in country A. In these cases, the plaintiff may try to enforce the judgment abroad. A special and complex set of rules has been developed for this purpose (see Born 1996). Some of these rules are included in bilateral or multilateral treaties, and they provide that – under certain conditions – judgments issued by the courts of one state must be enforced by the courts of the other states. In the absence of these rules, each country normally has domestic rules specifying under what conditions a foreign judgment may be enforced. These rules require, for example, that for a foreign judgment to be enforceable it should not be in violation of the public policy of the country where enforcement is sought, nor in violation of the mandatory jurisdiction rules of such country.

Defining the court that will decide a case is necessary to determine what rules will be applicable to such case. Each court uses its own conflicts of laws rules to decide, in cases with multinational elements, what national law is applicable to the case or to its different aspects. Conflict of laws rules vary from country to country, and therefore it is not possible to know which rules will be applied to a given case until a relevant conflict of laws system is used in connection with such case.

Parties may include contractual clauses choosing or determining the jurisdiction applicable to litigation arising in connection with the relevant contract. These clauses may determine one or more jurisdictions. The chosen jurisdictions may be *exclusive*, in the sense that the parties may not bring litigation regarding the contract in jurisdictions other than those indicated in the jurisdiction clause, or *non-exclusive*, in which case the parties may bring litigation before other jurisdictions, if there are grounds under the rules of such other jurisdictions to accept the case.

If a jurisdiction is thus chosen, it is still possible for the relevant courts to refuse the exercise of jurisdiction if the case does not have adequate contacts with the chosen forum, e.g. in countries having specialized courts, a civil case may not be transferred to a criminal court, even if the parties so agree.

In addition, if a jurisdiction is contractually chosen, other jurisdictions may not accept such choice, and thus may refuse to enforce judgments issuing from the chosen jurisdiction. This refusal may arise because the country where enforcement is sought has compulsory rules on jurisdiction, or because the courts of such country consider that the case does not have relevant contacts with the country whose courts have been chosen, or because the jurisdiction clause violates rules on consumer protection, or some other discrepancy.

A jurisdiction may also be chosen by the parties after a conflict has arisen between them. This type of agreement, however, is less common than the use of jurisdiction clauses in the context of contractual transactions.

Cases may also be decided through arbitration. Arbitration clauses may be included in a contract or may result from an agreement between conflicting parties aimed at deciding their conflict. The parties may submit the arbitration to a party chosen by them or else use one of the many institutional arbitration systems available throughout the world. Arbitration is often preferred due to its speed – as compared to normal court litigation – and cost, and also as a way to avoid electing a national court in the context of international transactions. However, this mode of conflict resolution has several limitations. Arbitrators have restricted powers and their awards have to be enforced through the state courts. Also, their decisions may be subject to different types of appeals before the state courts.

In the absence of an enforceable jurisdiction or arbitration clause, each country has a set of national rules determining the scope of its courts' jurisdiction. The methodology used with these rules is very different in the various countries of the world. Civil law countries tend to have relatively narrow and precise rules to determine their courts' jurisdiction, but once such jurisdiction is applicable they tend not to have mechanisms to limit its reach in favour of the courts of other countries that may also claim jurisdiction over the same case. The U.S., on the other hand, has rather broad rules on the reach of its courts' jurisdiction, but such courts may restrict the exercise of their jurisdiction if they consider that such exercise is inconvenient, e.g. because other courts are better placed to enforce an eventual judgment or to produce the relevant evidence of the case.

1.5 Special regulations on translation

There are many legal systems which include special regulations applicable to translations, particularly with regard to the professional practice of translators. These regulations are sometimes national in scope, while in other cases they have been enacted at the provincial or state level. In some countries, they result from the professional rules approved or adopted by guilds or professional associations; these rules may have legal effects and be enforceable as such, either because they are part of customary law or because there are statutes giving such guilds or association the power to sanction professional regulations.

Although the contents of these regulations vary among the different legal systems, they tend to include rules about the following matters:

- Requirements for the professional practice of translators, including university or other degrees, good conduct, examinations and legal capacity. These requirements are highly variable. It is common to require an official degree as a condition for the professional practice of translation or for entry into a professional guild or association. However, this type of requirement is sometimes impossible to satisfy for many languages, due to the lack of university or other courses on such languages; it is then replaced by special examinations or other mechanisms aimed at assuring that only qualified translators act as such. It should be pointed out that the result of this type of qualification requirements is that, in many countries, there are few or no authorized translators for many languages.

- Enrolment in a guild or association as a condition for the professional practice of translation. This enrolment may be subject to multiple requirements, such as payment of a yearly fee, passing certain examinations and satisfying certain degree and education requirements.
- Rules requiring that translations in general or those to be filed in court meet certain conditions, particularly being certified by a legally authorized translator. These requirements are often accompanied by other formalities, such as a certification of the translator's competence by the relevant guild or association. In some legal systems, courts have official lists of authorized translators and interpreters, and those acting in legal procedures must be chosen from these lists.
- Fee schedules. These schedules sometimes impose minimum fees, and in other cases, particularly those involving work in court, may determine the fees that the court will order as payable to translators or interpreters acting as experts or in other capacities in the context of litigation.
- Rules on ethics, confidentiality and other aspects of professional practice. The regulations described above may impose ethical standards on translators, as well as specific obligations regarding matters such as confidentiality and attribution of authorship.

1.6 Translations in court

The use of translations in judicial or administrative procedures is subject to special rules. These are highly variable from one jurisdiction to another, reflecting the fact that procedural rules are significantly different not only in different countries but even within the various jurisdictions or courts of the same national legal system.

Translations have a role in court procedures in the following cases:

- Translated documentation. Statutory provisions and procedural rules require that documentation, particularly that originated in other countries, should be translated into the national language or into the language used by the relevant court for such documentation to be valid and effective in the context of court procedures. These provisions and rules generally require that the translation be certified by a qualified translator. In some countries, the requirements are more complex; the certification by a qualified translator must in turn be certified by a translators' association or another authorized body, normally so as to determine that the translator has been authorized to act as such by that association or body or according to the rules governing the professional practice of translators.
- Expert witnesses. Translators may be called to act as expert witnesses in court, in connection with multiple issues. They may testify regarding

the accuracy of translations or regarding the meaning of certain foreign language documentation. In some countries, courts have official lists of authorized translators, who may be called upon to act as expert witnesses when the courts so require. These lists may be formed with voluntary applicants who must show that they have the necessary formal qualifications and who may be subject, in addition, to a screening procedure to determine their language skills. In addition, many legal systems allow the parties involved in court procedures to appoint their own expert witnesses for purposes of giving their professional opinion to the court in matters involving translation.
- Interpreters. Persons without knowledge of the language used by a court may appear as parties or witnesses before that court. These procedures require the participation of interpreters. Their participation is subject to multiple procedural rules, which vary among the different jurisdictions. Some systems require the interpreter to be sworn, after having been chosen and deemed qualified pursuant to the applicable rules of the court. Other systems apply to interpreters' rules similar to those applicable to expert witnesses, discussed above. A third group of jurisdictions have special requirements for court interpreters, who may be subject to special exams or to professional certifications by governmental or educational bodies or by translators' guilds or associations.

CASE STUDIES

A. XX, a translator domiciled in Spain, has entered into an agreement with M Co., a publisher located in the U.S., for the publication of a translation into English of a novel. The agreement includes a provision stating that any litigation resulting from such agreement will be submitted to the exclusive jurisdiction of the courts of Massachusetts. XX wishes to know whether this jurisdiction clause is valid, and which law will be applicable to a cause brought under the agreement.

Comments: The jurisdiction clause will normally be effective, if the case has some relevant contact with the jurisdiction whose courts have been chosen by the parties. However, it may still be possible for XX to appear before a different court, claiming that the contractual jurisdiction clause is invalid because it has been imposed by the publisher in the context of an *adhesion contract* – i.e. a standard-form contract prepared by one party to be signed by another, weaker, party, such as a consumer – or because it violates the public policy or compulsory jurisdiction of the country where such different court sits.

Only once the acting court has been defined will it be possible to decide what the law applicable to the case will be. The acting court will use its conflict of laws rules to decide whether its local laws or the law of a different jurisdiction are applicable. These conflict of laws rules tend to be significantly different when applied to contractual matters and to other issues. Regarding contractual matters, the conflict of law rules may base the definition of the applicable law on specific aspects of the relevant contract such as the place where the most characteristic obligation of the agreement is performed, or where the party performing such obligations has its domicile. Regarding matters related to copyright or intellectual property protection, the plaintiff will normally invoke the protection of the copyright or intellectual property laws of one or more countries, and the court will determine whether the protection granted by such laws covers the claims made by the plaintiff. This protection is based on territorial and other aspects of the conduct involved. The court will apply the local or foreign laws thus invoked, provided they do not violate the public policy of the country to which the court belongs.

B. Continuing with the facts described in A, XX also wishes to know whether the publisher can change the translation, upon its publication, from the version delivered by XX.

Comments: The answer will depend on what the applicable law is. Some countries, particularly those of the civil law tradition, grant "moral rights" in favour of the author. These moral rights – to be described in Chapter 2 – are not lost by the author through waiver or contractual provisions. Hence, if the translation falls within the reach of the copyright protection of one of these countries, the translator will be protected from unauthorized alterations of his or her work, at least within the territorial or other limits within which these national laws are applicable.

C. M, a multinational company, is engaged in litigation before the courts of Ruritania. The documentation to be presented by M in that litigation is in English. Ruritanian laws require that all foreign-language documentation presented before the courts of Ruritania be translated into Ruritanian. M wishes to know the practical implications of this requirement.

Comments: It will be necessary to determine whether Ruritania has a special regulatory regime applicable to translation. If it does, this regime may include rules determining what conditions must be satisfied by translated documents presented in the Ruritanian courts. These regimes will generally require that the translation be made and certified by an authorized translator. They may also determine what fees must be paid to the translator. In some legal systems, these fees are determined by the court acting in the case, using certain basic schedules included in the relevant regulations and taking into account other elements such as the importance and complexity of the documentation and the language involved.

2. Comparative and International Copyright Protection

2.1 Copyright and its legal significance for translations

Copyright is part of the intellectual property system. Intellectual property creates exclusive rights on intangibles. While traditional property implies an exclusive right over a physical object, such as land or movables, intellectual property consists of rights over goods that are not physically defined, but rather consist of ideas, expressions of ideas, distinctive signs and other conceptual elements. The limits of property on physical goods are defined on the basis of the physical characteristics of such goods. Using this type of legal mechanism, real estate rights refer to a piece of land having a certain location; other property rights may extend to specific movable goods or to an individual animal. The limits on intellectual property are defined on the basis of abstract elements, such as an idea, a given expression of an idea, or the distinctive characteristics of a sign. Intellectual property rights extend to conduct affecting objects having the characteristics defined by such rights. For instance, any item embodying a patented invention will imply a violation of the patent rights over such invention; there is no physical limit to the number and other characteristics of the infringing items, other than the fact that they include the different elements of the patented invention.

Intellectual property is traditionally divided into two branches: *industrial property* and *copyright*. This division does not follow strictly logical lines, but is rather the result of the historical development of intellectual property. Industrial property includes patents, designs, trademarks, trade names and other intangible goods generally related to technology or to distinctive signs. It is protected internationally by the Paris Convention and by the TRIPs Agreement. Copyright protects the expression of ideas; its coverage includes literary and musical works, among other intellectual creations. Copyright is protected internationally by the Berne Convention and by the TRIPs Agreement. In addition, a type of protection similar to that resulting from copyright is extended to the so-called *neighbouring rights*. These are intellectual property rights developed in connection with matters that do not strictly fall within the scope of copyright protection but are related to copyright. Neighbouring rights include the rights of performing artists, the rights of producers of phonograms, and the rights of broadcasting organizations; some countries protect other similar rights. Neighbouring rights are protected internationally by the Rome Convention and by the TRIPs Agreement.

Rights regarding a translation may be created and protected under several of these intellectual property mechanisms. A certain degree of protection may be obtained by a person producing or commissioning a translation by keeping the translation secret, in which case the national and international system of trade secret or know-how protection becomes applicable. However, copyright is the type of intellectual property whose contents and function are specifically framed to address the issues created by translations. Although copyright was originally created for the protection of literary and other works, and not specifically for translations, a set of rules specifically applicable to translations has been developed in its context. The copyright protection of translations results from the applicability to translations of the general copyright rules and from the specific rules focusing on the protection of translations. Copyright protects the intellectual content of translations against a broad array of conducts, which may affect the economic, intellectual or emotional value of such translations, such as the unauthorized reproduction or distribution of translations and the unauthorized publication of a previously unpublished translation. Copyright protection applies even in the absence of contractual arrangements; it extends both to published and unpublished works, and does not require the secrecy or confidentiality of the relevant information. The formal or bureaucratic requirements for copyright protection are generally few or non-existent, and the cost of such protection is therefore low.

Copyright protection, however, is not the only legal source of protection for translations. It is also possible to protect the rights of translators by means of confidentiality and contractual arrangements. These different types of protection are not mutually exclusive, but in some cases it may be necessary to choose one or the other. In particular, if a translator wishes to publish a translation, copyright protection is fully applicable, but publication negates any possibility of protection by means of confidentiality.

This chapter will examine the general rules of copyright, as determined by the applicable international conventions and by the national laws which implement such conventions. These general rules, when applied to translations, result in the specific copyright protection bearing on such translations, to be examined in the following chapters. That specific copyright protection is the result of the general copyright system, to be described in the following paragraphs. These paragraphs will include specific illustration of the relevance of general copyright rules for the protection of translations.

The general rules on copyright protection are also significant, for purposes of translation work, to determine the limits within which a translator may act without infringing another person's copyright. A translator will normally use dictionaries, software and other intellectual creations protected by copyright and will therefore need to know the limits within which she or he may act without infringing copyright on such intellectual works.

2.2 Copyright protection throughout the world

Copyright is protected by each national legal system. A copyright owner holds rights under each of the national legal systems granting copyright protection.

There is no world or international copyright; rather, a copyright owner holds a "bundle" of national rights.

However, these national copyright systems are not totally independent from each other. Several international treaties require that national copyright protection comply with certain minimum standards. This is the case, in particular, with the Berne Convention and the TRIPs Agreement. Most countries of the world are bound by these agreements, which do not create a uniform copyright system but do set certain minimum standards to be complied with by the member countries. These standards have resulted in a significant and increasing homogeneity between the different national copyright systems, at least from a theoretical point of view – enforcement is still radically different in the various national jurisdictions. In addition, certain groups of countries, such as the members of the European Union, are subject to bilateral or multilateral treaties that may determine, to some extent, the contents of their national copyright laws. However, the impact of these treaties is much less than that attributable to the Berne Convention and the TRIPs Agreement and to the effects of bilateral or regional treaties in other legal areas.

The Berne Convention,[1] which has been amended several times, includes minimum standards applicable to copyright protection. Most countries of the world have ratified this Convention. Its effectiveness has been greatly increased by the TRIPs Agreement.[2] Generally, a violation of the Berne Convention also constitutes a violation of the TRIPs Agreement, since the latter requires compliance with the Berne Convention, with some exceptions. The TRIPs Agreement includes minimum standards applicable to intellectual property protection, including copyright. It is part of the World Trade Organization agreements, which most countries of the world have ratified. A violation of the TRIPs Agreement may result in a procedure under a special mechanism for the settlement of disputes, governed by the rules of the World Trade Organization. If, under this mechanism, it is determined that there is a violation of the TRIPs Agreement, trade sanctions may be imposed on the country involved in such violation.

Under the Berne Convention – Article 5(1) – each country grants to the authors of the other member countries the same rights it grants to its own nationals. This rule, known as the national treatment rule, implies that a country may not discriminate between its own nationals and nationals of other member countries, with regard to copyright protection. An author protected under the Berne Convention has two types of basic rights in each of the Berne Convention countries: he or she will enjoy the minimum protection required by the Berne Convention and will have the same rights that each country grants to its own authors. Member countries of the Berne Convention may grant stronger

---

[1] On the Berne Convention, see Geller (2011).
[2] On the TRIPs Agreement, see Correa (2007).

copyright protection than that required by the Berne Convention – Article 19 – but in that case they have to extend the additional protection to all the nationals of Berne Convention countries. Thus, the author of a translation protected by copyright has a minimum set of rights in all the member countries of the Berne Convention, that is, practically, in most of the world.

For persons protected by the Berne Convention, copyright protection is granted, per Article 5(2), for all member countries of the Berne Convention without having to perform any formalities, such as registration or filings. This rule is extremely useful for authors and copyright owners, since it implies that protection is obtained throughout the world by the fact of being the author of a work or the assignee thereof. This is especially useful for translations, since many of them remain unpublished and do not justify the costs involved in worldwide registration. Registration and other formalities may be helpful for the author, particularly as evidence of authorship, but they are not necessary for copyright protection under the Berne Convention system. Oddly, this does not apply within the country of origin of the author, where it may still be necessary to record the work or perform other formalities. Thus, for example, an Argentine author obtains copyright protection in Argentina by recording his or her work in a special registry, but no such requirement may be imposed on Argentine authors outside Argentina, and Argentina may not impose such requirement on non-Argentine authors.

Although unified to some extent under the Berne Convention's and TRIPs Agreement's rules, copyright systems are still divided into two main groups. The copyright system based on the Anglo-American tradition[3] finds its origins in the British Statute of Anne, of 1710, and in the U.S. Constitution, particularly Article I, Section 8, Clause 8. Copyright is conceived as a property right, centred in the right to make copies, fully transferable under the same conditions as other rights of an economic nature.

The copyright systems based on the civil law tradition[4] find their origin in legislation enacted during the French Revolution. Emphasis is placed on the author's rights – rather than on the economic function of copyright – and this is reflected in the name used for this legal system in civil law countries, which is generally the equivalent of "authors' rights": *droit d'auteur* in French, *Urheberrecht* in German, *derecho de autor* in Spanish, etc. The original owner of copyright, in the civil law system, is the author. Copyright is viewed as including both economic and "moral" rights, the latter being necessarily linked to the author's personhood or identity and subject to limitations as to their waiver or transfer.

---

[3] On English copyright law, see Phillips, Durie and Whale (1997); on U.S. copyright law, see Nimmer and Nimmer (1997). A shorter description of U.S. copyright law is found in LaFrance (2008).

[4] Regarding copyright in civil law countries, see for example Dreier and Schulze (2006); Dessemontet (1999); Lipszyc (1993).

The different copyright systems are sufficiently homogeneous for certain basic characteristics common to them to be identified. These systems create certain exclusive rights in connection with intellectual works, including translations; these rights are subject to limitations of different types, such as the fair use doctrine applicable in the U.S. Different civil and criminal law remedies are provided for cases of infringement. These basic aspects of copyright will be described in the following paragraphs.

2.3 Protected works

Works protected by copyright are intellectual creations. Copyright does not protect specific physical objects but rather original intellectual creations. It grants exclusive rights regarding such creations, so that certain conduct related to a protected work is considered to be a copyright violation, e.g. the unauthorized reproduction of the protected work.

Copyright law defines protected works by means of two different mechanisms. It includes provisions stating in general terms that intellectual creations are protected by copyright, and it includes a list of protected works. The operative part of these provisions is the general definition they include. If a work is protected pursuant to the general definition of protected works, it will be legally protected even if it is not included in the list of specific protected works; this list is included for purposes of clarification.

Article 2(1) of the Berne Convention follows this methodology. It provides:

> The expression "literary and artistic works" shall include every production in the literary, scientific and artistic domain, whatever may be the mode or form of its expression, such as books, pamphlets and other writings, lectures, addresses, sermons and other works of the same nature; dramatic or dramatico-musical works; choreographic works and entertainments in dumb show; musical compositions with or without words; cinematographic works to which are assimilated works expressed by a process analogous to cinematography; works of drawing, painting, architecture, sculpture, engraving and lithography; photographic works to which are assimilated works expressed by a process analogous to photography; works of applied art; illustrations, maps, plans, sketches and three dimensional works relative to geography, topography, architecture and science.

The expression "such as", used in the third line of this provision, implies that works not included in the enumeration following that expression may still qualify as protected works. This has been the case, for example, with software, which became relevant many years after Article 2(1) of the Berne Convention was drafted.

In some cases, copyright laws indicate expressly that certain types of intellectual work are protected, or not, so as to avoid possible doubts on their legal status or to define more precisely the legal effects of the relevant protection. For instance, copyright statutes often include specific provisions indicating that software is protected. Article 2(3) of the Berne Convention provides that "(t)ranslations, adaptations, arrangements of music and other alterations of a literary or artistic work shall be protected as original works without prejudice to the copyright in the original work".

A basic rule when determining the general scope of the intellectual works protected by copyright is that the subject matter of copyright protection is the expression of an idea, and not the idea itself. Article 9(2) of the TRIPs Agreement states this rule: "Copyright protection shall extend to expressions and not to ideas, procedures, methods of operation or mathematical concepts as such". The exact meaning and practical consequences of this rule are vague and debatable. Procedures outlining how to obtain practical results are clearly beyond the scope of copyright protection; if such procedures are not protected by industrial property rights – e.g. patents – they may be used even if they have been described in a work which has copyright protection. It is the work – the expression of the procedure – and not the procedure itself – the "idea" – which is protected by copyright. Similarly, a mathematical algorithm cannot be protected by copyright – it is an "idea" – but a book describing and analysing such algorithm may be protected by copyright – it is an "expression" of the "idea". From this perspective, copyright differs from patent protection in that copyright protection extends to expressions, while patents give exclusive rights over inventions, which must consist of new procedures or products with functional characteristics. Copyright does not give exclusive rights over the functional characteristics of protected works.

In addition, copyright only applies to works which are original creations. This requirement encompasses two distinct aspects. First, for a work to be original it must be new, i.e. it must differ from preexisting works. In some countries, particularly the U.S., this requirement takes a different form, and originality is satisfied as long as two or more works are developed independently, even if they are fortuitously similar. Leaffer (1995:41–42), in the context of U.S. copyright law, states:

> An original work is one that is independently created, owing its origin to an author. Simply put, it is a work not copied from another. Courts have inferred the requirement of originality from the constitutional language which limits copyright to writings of authors. It follows that one can not be an author unless he originated something.

Second, the differences between the purportedly original work and other preexisting works must be such that the new work implies a process of artistic, scientific, literary or intellectual creation.

The originality requirements, although applicable to all types of subject matter protected by copyright, have different implications for each type of creation. Thus, for example, in the case of musical works, special emphasis has been placed on the melody; in the case of musical arrangements, a distinction has been introduced between "mechanical" and "creative" arrangements, only the latter being recognized as copyrightable derivative works, which have to include a minimum level of originality.

In a famous case – Feist Publications v. Rural Telephone Services (499 U.S. 340, 1991) – the U.S. Supreme Court rejected the "sweat of the brow" approach to copyright protection; protected works must possess a minimum degree of creativity, and the mere fact that substantial work is put into the development of a work – in this case a telephone directory – is not enough to make it copyrightable. The Court stated:

> To be sure, the requisite level of creativity is extremely low; even a slight amount will suffice. The vast majority of works make the grade quite easily, as they possess some creative spark, "no matter how crude, humble or obvious it might be".

The creativity requirement is applicable to translations, and has special relevance in this field, due to special characteristics of this type of work, which has both mechanical and creative aspects. The specific standards applicable to translations will be examined in Chapter 3.

Some countries include a "fixation" requirement. Thus under section 102(a) of the U.S. Copyright Act, original works are copyrightable if they are "fixed in any tangible medium of expression, now known or later developed, from which they can be perceived, reproduced, or otherwise communicated, either directly or with the aid of a machine or device". In these legal systems, fixation determines whether a work is copyrightable, as well as when copyright protection begins. However, Article 2(2) of the Berne Convention provides that it shall "be a matter for legislation in the countries of the Union to prescribe that works in general or any specified categories of works shall not be protected unless they have been fixed in some material form", and civil law countries, in general, do not apply fixation requirements. But even in these countries, fixation may be practically important, particularly for purposes of evidence and court procedures.

Certain aspects of intellectual works are generally excluded as relevant considerations for the definition of copyrightable works. Thus, the artistic, scientific, cultural or intellectual value or merit of a work is irrelevant to defining copyright protection, provided such work is original and implies a process of intellectual creation. If the originality requirements are satisfied, it is not for the courts or for the administrative authorities to weigh the value of the work; such assessment is left to the public. In the case of translations, the non-artistic or purely bureaucratic function of many of these works does not operate as an obstacle to their copyright protection.

Also, the purpose of the work is irrelevant to defining copyright protection. A work with a purely practical application may receive copyright protection. However, it is the expression of the intellectual work which is protected by copyright, and not the use to which the ideas included in such work may be put.

Similarly, the means or medium used for the expression or transmission of an intellectual work are irrelevant for purposes of defining copyright protection. If the nature of the work permits it, a given work may be expressed in different ways – orally, in writing, in electronic media, etc. – and each of these expressions will receive copyright protection.

Finally, there is no limit as to the types of intellectual work that may be protected, provided such work meets the general conditions described above; technically, this is referred to as the absence of a *numerum clausum*. If technology permits the development of new types of intellectual work – as has been the case with software – these new types of work will be protected provided they meet the general requirements applicable to all types of intellectual creations subject to copyright protection.

Certain possible substantive requirements for copyright protection have not yet been sufficiently defined in the different copyright systems. In particular, it is not clear whether "creations" made by machines, and not by humans, may be considered to be copyrightable works; this will be discussed in more detail, in the context of the copyright protection of translations in Chapter 3. Also, if a given expression is necessary to achieve certain practical results, as may be the case with certain software, it is debatable whether copyright protection is still admissible, since copyright would then create an exclusive right on the functional or technical aspects of the protected work. This is a problem that also has specific characteristics in the context of the copyright protection of translations, to be discussed in Chapter 3.

2.4 Categories of protected works

Copyright law has developed different categories of protected work, some of them directly included in national statutes and international treaties, and others resulting from case law or legal literature. These categories are not merely descriptive. Rather, the fact that a work falls into one or another of these categories has implications for the legal protection granted to that work.

It is common to distinguish between *original works* and *derivative works*. The former include literary, musical, theatrical, dramatic, artistic, scientific, audio-visual and software works, among others, that do not involve the alteration or modification of preexisting works. Derivative works include adaptations, translations, compilations, annotations, commentaries, summaries, extracts, musical arrangements and other transformations of preexisting works. Both groups of works are legally protected, although the type of protection varies for each category. The fact that translations are derivative works has important implications for the determination of the rules applicable to their copyright protection, as will be discussed in Chapter 3.

Article 2(3) of the Berne Convention provides that derivative works shall be protected as original works "without prejudice to the copyright in the original work". This implies that the derivative work can only be exploited by its author with the authorization of the owner of copyright in the original work, and that the owner of copyright in the original work can only exploit the derivative work with the authorization of the copyright owner of the derivative work. Also, a third party wishing to reproduce or otherwise exploit the derivative work must obtain the authorization of both the owner of the copyright in the original work and the owner of the copyright in the derivative work.

Generally, the different specific types of original works listed in provisions such as Article 2(1) of the Berne Convention (see paragraph 2.3 above) have the same type of copyright protection. However, this protection has some variations, in several cases, due to legal rules or to the specific characteristics of the works involved:

- Literary works. These include written and oral works. Protection covers both traditional literary production as well as other types of work implying a significant intellectual effort, such as slogans, nomenclatures, catalogues, forms, brochures, etc. The protection of oral works is supported by Article 2(1) of the Berne Convention. Collections of literary or artistic works, such as encyclopaedias and anthologies which, by reason of the selection and arrangement of their contents, constitute intellectual creations shall be protected as such, without prejudice to the copyright in each of the works forming part of such collection. This rule, included in Article 2(5) of the Berne Convention, implies that once a collection of protected works is formed, the same collection may not be reproduced without the authorization of the owner of copyright on such collection, but such owner needs the authorization of the copyright owners of the different works which form the collection, for purposes of reproducing or otherwise exploiting the collection.
- Musical works. Melody is considered to be the key element protected by copyright in this area. The determination of whether the limits of the protected elements of a musical work have been breached normally requires the help of expert witnesses.
- Theatrical works. These are considered to include theatrical works in their traditional form, as well as other intellectual works meant to be performed, such as choreographic works, even if these have not been described in writing or by means of pictures.

- Artistic works. These include paintings, drawings, engravings, sculpture, photography and architecture, but are not limited to these categories. A clear distinction is made in these cases between the protection of the artistic creation – regarding which copyright is granted – and the protection of the physical object – a painting, sculpture, etc., which embodies the artistic creation – which is governed by the rules on real property. Property of a physical object embodying an artistic creation grants no right to the reproduction or exhibition of that object or of the artistic creation embodied therein, which in principle belongs to the copyright owner.

  Generally, the artist is entitled to prevent any changes or modifications from being made to the work in the process of reproduction. However, in the case of architecture, the owner of the building is considered to be allowed to introduce changes for practical or technical reasons. With regard to photographs, they are clearly covered by copyright protection if they have an artistic value. The prevailing tendency is to admit copyright protection even in connection with photographs of a purely mechanical nature. Under Article 7(4) of the Berne Convention photographs are subject to special rules regarding the term of their copyright protection, which is determined by each country, but requiring a minimum period of twenty-five years from the making of the work, i.e. substantially less than for copyright protection in general.

  Artistic works with a practical or ornamental value may also be protected under other intellectual property rules, particularly those on industrial designs and models. Article 2(7) of the Berne Convention admits this possibility.
- Scientific works. They are protected to the extent that they result in the expression of a given theory, observation or scientific result. Scientific inventions, discoveries or projects are not protected by copyright, but their description is subject to copyright protection. Maps are protected, provided they involve an original expression by their author.
- Audiovisual works. Films and other audiovisual works are expressly covered by copyright protection. Special rules are usually included in copyright statutes regarding these works, particularly films. Thus, for example, Article 14(1) of the Berne Convention provides that authors of literary or artistic works shall have the exclusive right of authorizing the cinematographic adaptation and reproduction of these works, and the distribution of the works thus adapted or reproduced, and the public performance and communication to the public of the works thus adapted or reproduced. In these and other cases the exclusive right over communication of works currently includes communication by means of wire or cable, as well as wireless communication.

- Software. Article 10 of the TRIPs Agreement provides that computer programs, whether in source or object code, shall be protected as literary works under the Berne Convention. This copyright protection extends to the code and not to its functional characteristics. The code is treated as the expression of the functional aspects of the software. Many countries have enacted special provisions on software, due to the very specific legal issues it originates.
- Data compilations. Article 10 of the TRIPs Agreement also provides that compilations of data or other material, whether in machine readable or other form, which by reason of the selection or arrangement of their contents constitute intellectual creations shall be protected as such. Such protection, which shall not extend to the data or material itself, shall be without prejudice to any copyright subsisting in the data or material itself.

  The copyright protection of data compilations creates specific difficulties, particularly as to what constitutes intellectual creation in their context. Several countries include special provisions in the intellectual property rules to address these issues.

2.5 Works excluded from protection

Copyright statutes and treaties, such as the Berne Convention, set out positively the possible scope of copyright protection. They also include express provisions excluding certain intellectual works from such protection. On the basis of this methodology, works may be excluded from copyright protection for different reasons:

- Because they do not meet the substantive requirements for copyright protection. Thus, courts have traditionally decided that copyright protection does not extend to mere ideas; the expression of ideas is protected, but the subject matter of protection is the expression of the idea and not the idea itself. This general principle has been included in Article 9(2) of the TRIPs Agreement. Also, while courts will not evaluate the artistic or scientific merit of works, to determine whether they deserve copyright protection, a minimum level of creativity is always required, depending on the nature of the work for which protection is claimed.
- Because statutory rules provide that their subject matter is beyond the limits set for copyright protection. Thus, gambling procedures, game instructions, methods of operation, mathematical concepts and algorithms, among other intellectual tools, have been considered to be beyond the scope of copyright protection; Article 9(2) of the TRIPs Agreement includes provisions to this effect.

- Because a provision or legal principle excludes certain subject matter – which would otherwise be copyrightable – from protection. For different policy reasons, certain intellectual creations are not protected by copyright, even though they meet the substantive conditions normally required for intellectual property protection. Thus, some countries do not grant copyright protection to news of the day or to miscellaneous facts having the character of mere items of press information, and this exclusion is considered valid under Article 2(8) of the Berne Convention; political speeches and speeches delivered in the course of legal proceedings may also be excluded from copyright protection, under Article 2*bis*(1) of the Berne Convention. Expressions indicating or suggesting an official nature, such as "national", "official", "police", or words related to the armed forces, may be excluded from copyright protection, so as to prevent misleading expressions or work titles. Copyright may not extend to works prepared by an officer or employee of the government as part of his or her official duties, as is the case under section 105 of the U.S. Copyright Act.

It should be noted that a translation may be protected by copyright even if the original is excluded from protection, provided such translation meets the requirement for copyright protection. For example, the translation of a work which has fallen into the public domain because of expiration of the applicable term of protection is a separate work subject to copyright protection, provided it meets the general originality and creativity requirements.

2.6 Special categories of works

Copyright law has developed special rules applicable to certain categories of intellectual works. These works are thus governed by the general rules described in this chapter, and by the particular provisions applicable to each special category:

- Computer software. The appearance of computer programs created a lively debate as to whether they should be protected by copyright or by other legal means. The TRIPs Agreement took an express position on this matter, providing in its Article 10(1) that computer programs, whether in source or object code, shall be protected as literary works under the Berne Convention. This does not prevent individual countries from additionally protecting software by means of patents, as is the case with the U.S. The European Union refuses patent protection of software as such, although it may be patentable as part of a more complex invention. The different national copyright systems generally not only grant protection to software but include specific provisions

defining source and object code, listing special limitations on copyright in this area – e.g. the user's right to make safeguard copies – and providing special registration mechanisms to facilitate intellectual property protection.
- Databases. Article 10(2) of the TRIPs Agreements provides that compilations of data or other material, whether in machine readable or other form, which by reason of the selection or arrangement of their contents constitute intellectual creations shall be protected as such. Such protection, which shall not extend to the data or material itself, shall be without prejudice to any copyright subsisting in the data or material itself. Some countries provide a *sui generis* system for the protection of databases; this is the case with the European Union which, under European Council Directive 96/9/EC, grants certain exclusive rights regarding a database if it is shown that qualitatively or quantitatively a "substantial investment in either obtaining, verification or presentation of the contents" has been made. Other countries, such as the U.S., follow a copyright approach to database protection, requiring "intellectual creation", as is the case with other copyrightable works.
- Folklore. Difficulties in determining authorship, among other factors, have created a contemporary tendency towards enhancing protection of local folklore. This tendency is hampered, to some extent, by the rules of the Berne Convention and the TRIPs Agreement which disallow a more favourable differential treatment for local authors.
- Adaptations. To the extent that an adaptation is based on material protected by copyright, the authorization of the owner of such copyright must be obtained. The possible extent of the adaptation depends on the terms of the authorization given by the copyright owner. The author of an adaptation of a work which has fallen into the public domain – i.e. which is no longer the subject matter of copyright protection, particularly because of expiration of the term of protection – has an exclusive right on such adaptation but may not prevent other adaptations.
- Collections and anthologies. Under Article 2(5) of the Berne Convention, collections of literary or artistic works such as encyclopaedias and anthologies which, by reason of the selection and arrangement of their contents constitute intellectual creations, shall be protected as such, without prejudice to the copyright in each of the works forming part of such collections.
- Cinematographic works. Article 14*bis*(1) of the Berne Convention provides that, without prejudice to the copyright in any work which may have been adapted or reproduced, a cinematographic work is protected as an original work, and the owner of copyright in a cinematographic work shall enjoy the same rights as the author of an original work. The Berne Convention allows individual countries to provide special

rules of their choice as to the determination of copyright ownership on cinematographic works.
– Journalistic publications. Unsigned articles, reports, interviews, drawings, engravings and general information included in a journal, magazine or periodical publication are generally considered to be the property of the publisher of such a journal, magazine or periodical, unless they have been acquired from a third party, provided they are original. The authors of signed articles, reports, interviews and other journalistic material are the owners of the intellectual property rights on such material. Press information consisting of news of the day or miscellaneous facts may be excluded from copyright protection, in accordance with Article 2(8) of the Berne Convention.

Translations are also subject to special copyright rules, to be described in Chapter 3.

2.7 Formal requirements

The general rule is that the enjoyment and exercise of copyright is not subject to any formality. This general rule is fully applicable to the copyright protection of translations. It is included in Article 5(2) of the Berne Convention, but it is subject to certain limits and qualifications.

Copyright arises by virtue of the creation of an original work; some countries, such as the U.S., require, in addition, that the work be fixed in some material form. However, some countries also require registration of the work for the exercise of certain rights. Thus, for example, in the case of published works, the exclusive right of the editor resulting from copyright may only be exercised if the work has been registered in an official registry. If the country is member of the Berne Convention – as most countries are – this type of requirement is only applicable to works whose country of origin is the country where registration is required. In other words, Article 5(2) of the Berne Convention prevents the extension of registration and other formal requirements to foreign authors.

The Berne Convention system as to formal requirements implies an enormous advantage for the protection of authors. An author may obtain protection practically throughout the world, without incurring the cost and complications resulting from registration and other formal requirements. This is especially important for translators, due to the highly variable individual value of their works and the cost that registration would imply. However, registration may still be convenient, for several reasons.

First, registration may be necessary in the country of origin of the work, and this requirement is not invalidated by the Berne Convention.

Second, registration may be convenient for purposes of evidence. The fact that a work is registered may be used as evidence of authorship or ownership, and create a rebuttable presumption of validity of the copyright claimed through that registration.

Third, registration may be required to obtain certain types of legal protection, e.g. protection against imports of illegal copies.

Finally, registration may be necessary to participate in compulsory licensing systems and to derive royalties therefrom. These licensing systems allow users of protected works to copy or otherwise use such works, without the copyright owner's authorization, with the obligation to pay a royalty administered by a body in charge of the system.

Registration procedures vary from country to country. Generally they include filing a form, depositing copies of the protected work and paying a fee. Registration is normally automatic, i.e. it is not subject to a screening or approval procedure.

Some countries impose formal requirements different from or additional to registration; e.g. affixing a copyright notice to published or distributed works, or making a deposit of the material to be protected by copyright in public libraries and other governmental agencies. But, under Article 5(2) of the Berne Convention these requirements are also inapplicable as a condition for the enjoyment and exercise of copyright, at least for works with a country of origin other than that in which the formal requirements are imposed.

Registration, when applicable, normally takes place in a government-run institution. Special rules govern access to these registries, for example, in cases in which evidence from the registered materials must be presented in court. In some countries there are special registries for certain types of works, such as software.

Registration and formal requirements may be imposed in connection with transactions related to copyright, such as licences and other transactions through which the exploitation of the work is authorized, transactions assigning or modifying copyright, etc. Generally, the registration of these transactions is not necessary for the transaction to be considered valid or for the underlying copyright to be effective. However, lack of registration may allow third parties, such as creditors of the assignor, to disregard the transaction until it is registered, and unregistered copyright may have negative tax effects, such as not permitting a licensee to deduct royalties paid under an unregistered agreement from taxable profits.

2.8 Ownership

The general rule is that copyright ownership belongs to the author. Article 2(6) of the Berne Convention follows this approach, stating that copyright protection "shall operate for the benefit of the author and his successor in title". This general rule applies to translations; for these purposes the author of the translation – as distinguished from the author of the translated original – is the translator who performs the translation work. The identification of the translator as author will be described in Chapter 3.

Ownership of copyright in a work is separate from ownership of the physical embodiment of such work. Copyright ownership is based on intellectual authorship, and the intellectual work thus created may result in multiple physical embodiments, each of them subject to specific rules on tangible property which do not affect the copyright in the intellectual creation. For instance, once a book is published each individual copy will circulate according to the rules on tangible property, which are different from the copyright rules which determine whether publication was valid from an intellectual property perspective.

In civil law countries, the general rule of copyright ownership by the author has stronger implications than in countries of the Anglo-American tradition. Since authorship implies an intellectual creation, and this in turn requires a human activity, civil laws countries base their ownership rules on the idea that only individuals, and not corporations or other legal entities, may be the original owners of copyright. However, even in civil law countries there are certain exceptions to the rule that corporations or other legal entities may not be the original owners of copyright. Anonymous collective works may be considered to belong immediately to the institutions, corporations or other legal entities which organized such collective works. With regard to works made for hire or resulting from an employment relationship, they may be considered to be immediately transferred to the employer. Strictly speaking, the original owner of the copyright is still the individual who created the underlying work, but the economic content of such copyright is immediately transferred to the employer. The distinction is important because it bears on issues such as the duration of copyright and the so-called moral rights, to be discussed in 2.14.

Countries of the Anglo-American tradition are more open to the possibility of immediate and original ownership of copyright by a person other than the intellectual author. Thus, in cases of work made for hire, the party that employed or commissioned the intellectual author is the original owner of copyright under section 201(b) of the U.S. Copyright Act, and that party owns the copyright free of the intellectual author's rights.

In addition to these general rules, different special rules have been developed in connection with certain categories of intellectual works:

- Translators have a separate individual right on their translation, even if it refers to a translated work which has fallen into the public domain, without prejudice to the copyright in the original work. This rule will be examined in more detail in Chapter 3. Similar rules apply to adaptations, arrangements of music and other alterations of protected works, pursuant to Article 2(3) of the Berne Convention.

- In cases of musical works including wording, the music and the words are two different works which may belong to two separate individual original authors.
- In the case of anonymous works, copyright may belong to the editor or publisher, but the anonymous author may at any time claim the copyright by showing his or her identity and authorship.
- In the case of cinematographic works, Article 14*bis*(2)(a) of the Berne Convention allows individual countries to determine the copyright ownership. Thus, the owners may be the authors who have brought contributions to the making of the work – a possibility dealt with by Article 14*bis*(2)(b) of the Berne Convention – or the producers, or a combination thereof, among other possibilities.
- In cases involving collections, encyclopaedias and anthologies, the author of the selection and arrangement of the contents owns the rights to such intellectual work, without prejudice to the copyright in each of the works forming part of such collections, encyclopaedias and anthologies.

2.9 Works created by several persons

Special rules on copyright ownership apply in connection with works created by several persons. Copyright law has developed several categories to deal with the issues created by the variety and complexity of the joint creative process. These rules and categories are applicable to translations performed by several persons.

Works done through cooperation imply a creative collaboration between different authors. Such authors do not merely add the results of their creative efforts, but rather direct and organize their work with a view towards a common result. Cooperation is defined as "perfect" if the resulting work is indivisible, and "imperfect" if it is possible to distinguish the results attributable to each coauthor. U.S. law uses the terminology "joint work", which is defined by Section 101 of the Copyright Act as "a work prepared by two or more authors with the intention that their contributions be merged into inseparable or independent parts of a unitary whole". U.S. law distinguishes between "interdependent" contributions, where each element has some meaning or value standing alone, and "inseparable" contributions, where the elements contributed by each author cannot be separated into units with independent creative value. With different terminologies, similar distinctions may also be found in civil law countries.

A different category is that of collective works. Some legal systems characterize these works as those created through the initiative or direction of one or more individuals, who coordinate or direct the efforts of several other individuals so as to achieve a joint result; collective works include works such as dictionaries, encyclopaedias, compilations, etc. Under U.S. law the following distinction is made between joint works and collective works (LaFrance 2008:79):

> A joint work also differs from a collective work, in which each author's creative contribution stands on its own as an independent copyrightable work. Unlike the authors of a joint work, the authors of the individual works that are combined into a collective work do not intend to merge their contributions as inseparable or interdependent parts of a single unitary work. Rather, they intend for their individual contributions to retain their identities as separate copyrightable works. Each author owns the copyright in his or her individual contribution, and the compiler is the author and copyright owner of the collective work.

Collective works and joint works are also distinguished from composite works; these are the result of adding separate works, which were created as potentially independent works, each one with a possible separate author and owner, into one final result. This result may take place after a considerable time has elapsed after the creation of each or some of the original separate works. Composite works include but are not limited to translations, adaptations and music with words. For instance, a novel which is then used as the basis for a cinematographic work had an original independent value and then becomes part of a composite work. But a contribution to an encyclopaedia is part of collective work, since it was created with the intention of its being part of such encyclopaedia.

These different categories are not merely descriptive of certain legal relationships, but rather have significant legal consequences, which vary from one legal system to another. In the case of collective works, it is relatively straightforward to determine each author's share in the copyright in the collective work. There is an author for each individual work, forming part of the collective work, and also an author of the collective work as a whole, and each of these authors has the original right on his or her work, which may then be assigned or transferred to other persons on the basis of the rules on works made for hire – such rules are discussed in paragraph 2.10 – or by means of contracts. In the case of joint works, the various authors may have different degrees of participation in the joint work. One possibility is to grant each author the same proportional participation in the economic rights related to the work, while other systems allow the possibility of assigning different proportional participation on the basis of the importance of each joint author's contribution.

Another significant difference lies in the authorization necessary for the exploitation of these works. In the case of collective works, each coauthor may exploit separately the elements he or she has contributed to the collective work, and authorize a similar exploitation by third parties, in both cases provided no damage is caused to the work as a whole or to the rights related thereto. Consequently, the consent of all the co-authors, as well as the authorization of the owner of copyright in the collective work as a whole, would be necessary for the exploitation of the collective work, including its constituent elements. A similar rule applies to composite works, although some exceptions are applicable for some specific types of work, such as cinematographic works, regarding which it is possible to exclude the authorization of the author of the script or of the music – among other possible authors – as a legal requirement to the exhibition or other uses of the film (see Berne Convention, art. 14*bis*(2) (b)). With regard to joint works, some legal systems – such as the U.S.'s – allow each co-owner to use or license the whole work, with the obligation to account for profits to the other co-owners, but require the consent of all the co-owners for purposes of assigning copyright in the work or granting exclusive licences thereto. Other systems require the consent of all the co-authors for the exploitation and license of copyright.

2.10 Works made for hire

Works made for hire include works made by employees acting within the scope of their employment, and works that have been specially ordered or commissioned. A large proportion of translation works fall in this category. The different legal systems apply special rules to allocate copyright on these works.

In the case of works made by employees, not all the works developed by such employees in the course of their employment belong to the employer. Generally, all legal systems grant copyright to the employer if the employee was expressly hired to undertake creative activities from which copyrightable works result. In addition, some legal systems may grant copyright to the employer if it controls the manner and means by which the work is created, or if the work is developed on the basis of intellectual property previously belonging to the employer, in both cases even if the employee was not hired to develop or create certain works. Intellectual property regimes also recognize – with variable definitions – an area of "independent" creations that belong to the employee, particularly when they are unrelated to the employee's employment scope; e.g. a scientist who writes novels in his or her spare time. The rules applicable to works made by employees will be examined in more detail in Chapter 5.

If works are made for hire in circumstances which do not involve employment relationships, the property rights on such works will depend on the contractual terms agreed by the parties. The different legal systems include restrictions on the effects of contractual terms as to transferring copyright from the author. Thus, under Section 101 of the U.S. Copyright Act, works created by independent contractors do not qualify as works made for hire unless they are "specially ordered or commissioned for use as a contribution to a collective work, as a part of a motion picture or other audiovisual work, as a translation, as a supplementary work, as a compilation, as an instructional text, as a test, as answer material of a test, or as an atlas". In addition U.S. law requires a written agreement unambiguously reflecting the intent that the work involved be a work made for hire. Other legal systems provide that an intellectual work supplied by the author with a specific purpose, e.g. an architectural plan, gives the acquirer the right to put that work to its normal intended use, but not the copyright in general, nor the right to reproduce or otherwise exploit such work in connection with third parties, in the absence of express provisions stating otherwise.

2.11 Assignments and licences

Copyright – including copyright on translations – can be the subject of assignments, licences and other legal transactions, such as donations. The legal consequence of an assignment is that the assigned copyright is transferred to the assignee, while a licence means that the licensor retains the copyright but authorizes the exploitation or use of the subject matter of such copyright.

The general rule is that all the elements of copyright may be assigned by their owner, except in cases in which a rule prohibits or limits the assignment. The following prohibitions and limits on copyright assignment may be mentioned:

- The assignment is valid only for the term provided by law for the copyright subject to assignment. Strictly speaking, this is not a limitation of the assignment but rather simply an application of the rule that an assignor may not extend, by means of the assignment, the scope or duration of the rights previously held by such assignor.
- In civil law systems, the assignment may only extend to the economic or exploitation rights, and not to the author's moral rights. In particular, the author retains the right to have his or her work properly reproduced, and to have his or her name mentioned in connection with the assigned work.
- The assignee may be subject to legal restrictions on the possibility of changing the title, form or contents of the work.
- While it is possible to assign the rights to specific future works, some legal systems prohibit the general assignment of the rights to all the future intellectual production of the author, on the basis that such general assignment would jeopardize the author's incentive to create intellectual works.
- Clauses providing that the assignor may not obtain copyright in the future with respect to new works or that prohibit the assignor from

creating new intellectual works are considered void in some legal systems.

Various countries provide that copyright assignments, to be fully legally effective, must be registered with a government agency. This requirement often implies that an unregistered assignment will not be void, but rather only invalid with relation to bona fide third parties, e.g. the assignor's creditors; the agreement will still be valid between the assignor and the assignee.

With regard to licences, it is necessary to distinguish between complex contracts which include a copyright licence as part of a broader transaction, and licences granted under the general contract law rules. Copyright law includes special provisions on some of the aforementioned complex contracts. The typical case is a publishing agreement. This agreement implies that the copyright owner retains such ownership, unless a contractual provision to the contrary is agreed. The publisher acquires the right to reproduce, distribute and sell the work; the extent and limits of these rights may be contractually arranged between the parties. The publisher is therefore a licensee of the relevant copyright, but both the publisher and the copyright owner are subject to multiple other legal obligations in the context of the publishing agreements, such as collaborating in the editing process and distributing a certain number of copies of the published work.

Other complex licences are part of agreements such as performance agreements and audiovisual works production agreements. In performance agreements an author or its assignors or successors agrees to deliver to an entrepreneur a theatrical work for public performance and such work is accepted by the entrepreneur, who generally undertakes to have it performed. In audiovisual works production agreements an author of a literary, dramatic or artistic work authorizes its inclusion by a producer in an audiovisual work, such as a film, which will be distributed and exhibited by the producer.

Licences may be exclusive or non-exclusive. An exclusive licence exists when the licensor undertakes not to grant other licences within the scope of the exclusive licence. Non-exclusive licences permit additional competing licences. Exclusive and non-exclusive licences may be subject to different rules under certain legal systems; e.g. as to the requirement that the licence be in writing. An additional distinction is made between weak exclusive licences – in which the licensor agrees not to grant other licences but retains the right to exploit the work subject to the licence – and strong exclusive licence – in which the licensor agrees, in addition, not to exploit the licenced work himself or herself; weak exclusive licences are sometimes called sole licences.

2.12 Exclusive rights

Copyright consists of a set or bundle of exclusive rights on an intellectual work. These rights constitute what is technically called a *ius prohibendi*, i.e.

the right to prohibit certain conduct in connection with the subject matter of the right. Thus, for example, the copyright owner may have the right to prohibit the unauthorized reproduction of the work.

Exclusive rights are subject to various restrictions and limitations, to be described in paragraph 2.16.

The rights which are part of copyright are traditionally divided into economic or exploitation rights, and moral rights. Although this distinction was developed by and is typical of civil law system, it is now universal, since it has been adopted by the Berne Convention. Exploitation and moral rights will be described in the following paragraphs.

2.13 Economic or exploitation rights

Economic or exploitation rights imply an exclusive right to exploit and profit from the protected work by placing such work on the market or distributing copies of such work. Generally, the national copyright systems specify or list these rights; however, to some extent they also recognize a general exploitation right, such that all acts of economic exploitation of a protected work belong exclusively to the copyright owner, even in connection with types of exploitation not envisaged by the applicable statutes. This possibility is especially significant because of the permanent changes in the types of exploitation that become technically feasible.

Exploitation rights are defined by each national copyright system. However, certain minimum exploitation rights are required by the Berne Convention, and are therefore found in the legal systems of most countries of the world. The following exploitation rights may be mentioned:

- Reproduction right. Article 9(1) of the Berne Convention provides that "(a)uthors of literary and artistic works protected by this Convention shall have the exclusive right of authorizing the reproduction of these works, in any manner or form." More generally, the copyright owner's reproduction right applies to all types of works protected by copyright – including translations – and to any form of reproduction of such works. The copyright owner has an exclusive right to reproduce the relevant work by means such as printing, drawings, engravings, photographs, photocopies, microfilms, films, tapes, disks, electronic formats, etc. Any type of unauthorized reproduction of the protected intellectual work constitutes a violation of copyright, with the exceptions to be described in paragraph 2.16. No reproduction of the work is legally valid without the copyright owner's consent. Such consent takes place by means of a licence or authorization. The consent for reproduction may be extended with respect to limited copies or instances of reproduction, or in an unlimited way. It may refer to specific parts

- of a given work, or extend only to certain media of expression, or be limited to a given geographical area.
- Performance rights. Under Article 11 of the Berne Convention, authors of dramatic, dramatico-musical and musical works shall enjoy the exclusive right of authorizing the public performance of their works – including such public performance by any means or process – and any communication to the public of the performance of their works. Authors of dramatic or dramatico-musical works shall enjoy, during the full term of their rights in the original works, the same rights with respect to translations thereof. National copyright systems often extend performance rights to all types of copyrightable works, within the limits set by the physical or intellectual nature of the work involved. Also, copyright rules include all types and means of performance within the scope of these rights. Performance rights have been considered to include the following types of performance, without prejudice to other possible types of performance which may be developed on the basis of new techniques and which would also be encompassed by copyright: exhibition of artistic works, either by means of the original or through films, television or other means; scenic performance of dramatic, musical, choreographic or theatrical works; readings and recitals of literary works; conferences, lectures or sermons; public performances by means of mechanical instruments, particularly in the case of musical works; radio and television transmissions; satellite broadcasting; cable transmissions; public access to databases or other elements stored by electronic means, etc.
- Rental rights. These rights imply that, even after a copy of a work has been lawfully put into circulation with the copyright owner's authorization, such owner retains the exclusive right to authorize the rental of such work. In connection with rental rights, Article 11 of the TRIPs Agreement provides:

In respect of at least computer programs and cinematographic works, a Member (country) shall provide authors and their successors in title the right to authorize or to prohibit the commercial rental to the public of originals or copies of their copyrighted works. A Member shall be excepted from this obligation in respect of cinematographic works unless such rental has led to widespread copying of such works which is materially impairing the exclusive right of reproduction conferred in that Member on authors and their successors in title. In respect of computer programs, this obligation does not apply to rentals where the program itself is not the essential object of the rental.

- Broadcasting and related rights. Article 11*bis* of the Berne Convention provides that the authors of literary and artistic works shall enjoy the exclusive right of authorizing the broadcasting of their works or the

communication thereof to the public by any other means of wireless diffusion of signs, sounds or images; any communication to the public by wire or by rebroadcasting of the broadcast of the work, when this communication is made by an organization other than the original one; and the public communication by loudspeaker or any other analogous instrument transmitting, by signs, sounds or images, the broadcast of the work. National copyright laws extend these rights to other types of copyrightable works.
- Right of translation. Article 8 of the Berne Convention requires that authors of literary and artistic works have the exclusive right of making and of authorizing the translation of their works throughout the term of protection of their rights in their original works. This right will be examined in more detail in Chapter 3.
- Right of public recitation. Article 11*ter* of the Berne Convention provides that authors of literary works shall enjoy the exclusive right of authorizing the public recitation of their works, including such public recitation by any means or process, and any communication to the public of the recitation of their works. In addition, they shall enjoy, during the full term of their rights in the original works, the same right with respect to translations thereof.
- Right of adaptation. The exclusive right of authorizing adaptations, arrangements and other alteration of literary or artistic works is provided in favour of their authors by Article 12 of the Berne Convention. National laws extend these rights to all types of protected works. The copyright owner may decide to make adaptations himself or herself, or else authorize third parties to make such adaptations. In the case of such authorization, the adaptation must comply with the limits set by the author of the original work. The author of the original work and of the adaptation will share rights as coauthors of the adapted work. If the owner of an original work authorizes its adaptation, he or she may still authorize new and different adaptations, and different sets of rights will apply to each separate adaptation.
- Other economic rights. Other economic rights are granted by some copyright systems. French law, as well as other national legislations, grants the so called *droit de suite*; the Berne Convention – Article 14*ter* – defines this right, but allows each member country to grant it or not. Article 14*ter*(1) of the Berne Convention provides that this right has the effect that:

The author, or after his death the persons or institutions authorized by national legislation, shall, with respect to original works of art and original manuscripts of writers and composers, enjoy the inalienable right to an interest in any sale of the work subsequent to the first transfer by the author of the work

Thus, for example, if sculptor XX sells a sculpture to Ms. YY, if YY subsequently sells such sculpture, XX will have the right to participate in the proceeds of such subsequent sale, pursuant to the provisions of the laws of the country whose *droit de suite* is applicable to such sale.

- Some countries also recognize public distribution rights – i.e. the right to distribute copies of the work to the public and to authorize such distributions –, public lending rights – i.e. the exclusive right to lend copies of the work to the public –, public display rights – i.e. the exclusive right to publicly display a copy of the work –, among other possible economic or exploitation rights.

2.14 Moral rights

Moral rights were developed by civil law countries, particularly by French law, but are nowadays part of the world copyright system, their protection being required by Article 6*bis* of the Berne Convention. Paragraph (1) of Article 6*bis* provides:

> Independently of the author's economic rights, and even after the transfer of said rights, the author shall have the right to claim authorship of the work and to object to any distortion, mutilation or other modification of, or other derogatory action in relation to, the said work, which would be prejudicial to his honor or reputation.

Moral rights are derived from the idea that an intellectual work is linked to the personhood of its author, and that this author is always an individual, acting alone or with other individuals. On this basis, affecting the identity and other aspects of a work also affects its author, either emotionally or as to such author's honour or reputation.

Countries of the Anglo-American tradition did not originally recognize or protect moral rights; thus, U.S. federal copyright law contained no explicit moral rights provisions until 1990. However, moral rights are protected by the Berne Convention system, and participation in this system has meant that most countries of the world protect or have the obligation to protect moral rights. Moral rights are part of the copyright protection of translations.

The following moral rights may be mentioned:

- A right of integrity, consisting in the right to preserve the text, title and other contents of the work, even if property rights on such work have been assigned.
- A right of attribution, consisting in the right to have the author named and identified together with the work.

- A right of divulgation, consisting in the right to decide whether the work will be published or not. Normally this right only applies for as long as the author has not taken the decision to publish the work. Once the author authorizes publication, such author is bound by his or her decision.
- A right to withdraw the work from circulation. Only some countries grant this additional right, which alters the effect of the aforementioned right of divulgation.
- A right to modify the work, even after it has been published. Again, only some countries grant this right, which goes beyond the right of integrity.

Moral rights extend after the death of the author; under Article 6*bis*(2) of the Berne Convention they must be maintained, at least, until the expiry of the economic rights, and shall be exercisable, after the author's death, by the persons or institutions defined by each country.

Although moral and economic rights generally arise simultaneously, and in favour of the author, they exist independently from each other. Economic or exploitation rights may be transferred, but the author will retain his or her moral rights. These are considered to be non-assignable. They may not be waived or surrendered in a general way, although they may be waived in connection with specific conducts or situations.

Moral rights extend to all types of copyrightable works, even those such as software in which the "personal" element is weak. However, they have special features and are subject to special restrictions in connection with certain types of work, such as cinematographic works.

Although moral rights are required by the Berne Convention, their extent and enforcement varies significantly among the different legal systems. The TRIPs Agreement excludes moral rights from the obligations on copyright protection included in that Agreement, thus making the international enforcement of moral rights weaker. In the U.S., in particular, the statutory protection of moral rights is not clearly established and such rights are construed more narrowly than in civil law jurisdictions.

2.15 Term of protection

Copyright protection has a limited duration. Generally, the term of protection is calculated on the basis of the author's life. Thus, under Article 7(1) of the Berne Convention the term of protection shall be the life of the author plus fifty years after his or her death. Many countries, however, grant longer terms of protection; for instance, seventy years after the author's death under French law.

Regarding certain works or types of authorship, both the Berne Convention and the national laws provide specific rules. Thus:

- Under Article 7(2) of the Berne Convention, in the case of cinematographic works, the term of protection expires fifty years after the work has been made available to the public with the consent of the author, or failing such an event within fifty years from the making of such work, fifty years after its production.
- Under Article 7(3), in the case of anonymous or pseudonymous works, the term of protection shall expire fifty years after the work has been lawfully made available to the public.
- In the case of photographic works and works of applied art protected as artistic works, countries subject to the Berne Convention rules must grant a term of protection running at least until the end of a period of twenty-five years from the making of such a work (Article 7(4)).
- Article 8 provides that in the case of a work of joint authorship, the terms measured from the death of the author shall be calculated from the death of the last surviving author.

2.16 Limitations on and exemptions from copyright protection

Copyright laws impose multiple limitations on the economic and moral exclusive rights granted to authors. Article 9 of the Berne Convention includes a basic provision, in relation to the right of reproduction – described in paragraph 2.13 above – authorizing member countries to permit the reproduction of works protected by copyright "in certain special cases, provided that such reproduction does not conflict with a normal exploitation of the work and does not unreasonably prejudice the legitimate interests of the author". This broad standard is also applied with relation to possible limitations on and exemptions from other exclusive rights.

Different legal concepts are used in the national copyright laws for purposes of implementing the limitations on and exemptions from copyright protection. Thus U.S. law includes a number of concrete statutory limitations and exemptions, as well as a general defence to actions for copyright infringement, called the *fair use doctrine*. The fair use doctrine has been defined[5] as a "privilege in others than the owner of a copyright to use the copyrighted material in a reasonable manner without his consent, notwithstanding the monopoly granted to the owner". The fair use doctrine seeks to limit the reach of the exclusive rights of the copyright owner, where the normal or statutory extension of such rights would unduly or disproportionately restrict the use of copyrighted material, with unjustified detriment to creativity and to the use and circulation

---
[5] Rosemont Enterprises, Inc. v. Random House, Inc., 366 F.2d 303, 306 (2d. Cir. 1966), cert. denied, 385 U.S. 1009 (1967).

of intellectual works. The fair use doctrine is fully applicable to translations and to the scope of their copyright protection.

Although the U.S. Copyright Act does not include a general definition of fair use, it does provide, in its section 107, a list of factors to be considered in determining whether the use made of a work in any particular case is a fair use, namely:

- The purpose and character of the use, including whether such use is of a commercial nature or is for nonprofit educational purposes. Section 107 lists certain purposes for which the use of a copyrighted work may be fair "such as criticism, comment, news reporting, teaching (including multiple copies for classroom use), scholarship, or research".
- The nature of the copyrighted work. Generally, fair use is applied more restrictedly in connection with works embodying a high level of creativity.
- The amount and substantiality of the portion used in relation to the copyrighted work as a whole.
- The effect of the use upon the potential market for or value of the copyrighted work.

Although the fair use doctrine is famously vague, its legal effects are relatively foreseeable due to the abundant case law, in the U.S., regarding its consequences and limits. Section 107 of the U.S. Copyright Act mentions, as possible legitimate purposes in the use of copyrighted works, "criticism, comment, news reporting, teaching (including multiple copies for classroom use), scholarship, or research". This is not an exhaustive list. Also, fair use is determined not only by the existence of a legitimate purpose but also by other aspects of the relevant use, such as its economic effects.

Civil law countries tend to provide in their laws specific limitations and exemptions; these commonly reflect certain provisions of the Berne Convention authorizing limitations and exceptions, but also result from the broader authorization of limits on the right of reproduction included in Article 9 of the Berne Convention and in the TRIPs Agreement. The following rules of the Berne Convention may be mentioned in this context:

- Article 2(4) allows the member countries to exclude official texts of a legislative, administrative and legal nature, and official translations of such texts, from copyright protection.
- Article 2(8) excludes news of the day or miscellaneous facts having the character of mere items of press information from copyright protection under the Berne Convention.
- Article 2*bis*(1) allows the exclusion from protection of political speeches and speeches delivered in the course of legal proceedings.

- Article 2*bis*(2) permits member countries to allow the reproduction by printing and other media of lectures, addresses and other works of the same nature which are delivered in public, when such use is justified by its informatory purpose.
- Article 10(1) declares it permissible to make quotations from a work which has already been lawfully made available to the public, provided that their making is compatible with fair practice, and their extent does not exceed that justified by the purpose, including quotations from newspaper articles and periodicals in the form of press summaries.
- Article 10(2) allows member countries to permit the utilization, to the extent justified by the purpose, of literary or artistic works by way of illustration in publications, broadcasts or sound or visual recordings for teaching, provided such utilization is compatible with fair practice.
- Article 10*bis*(1) allows member countries to permit the reproduction by the printing, the broadcasting or the communication to the public by wire of articles published in newspapers or periodicals on current economic, political or religious topics, and of broadcast works of the same character, in cases in which the reproduction, broadcasting or such communication thereof is not expressly reserved.
- Article 10*bis*(2) allows member countries to permit the reproduction and distribution to the public, for the purpose of reporting current events by means of photography, cinematography, broadcasting or communication to the public by wire, of literary or artistic works seen or heard in the course of the event.
- Certain special restrictions are permitted in connection with musical and cinematographic works.

On the basis of these provisions, and particularly of the authorization of restrictions on the right of reproduction included in Article 9 of the Berne Convention, described at the beginning of this paragraph, national laws frequently include other limitations on and restrictions from copyright protection, such as the following:

- Private copies for personal use and the private use of protected work are often considered not to be in violation of the copyright which may exist with regard to the copied work.
- Once a copy of a work is lawfully made and sold, it can circulate freely in the market without infringing the copyright on such work; this general rule is called the *first sale rule* in the U.S. and the *exhaustion doctrine* in the European Union.
- National laws grant certain exemptions for the use of works for educational purposes. These rules allow, for example, the inclusion of up to a certain number of words as part of educational works without requiring the authorization of the author of such excerpt.

- Libraries and archives enjoy in some countries an exception allowing them to reproduce and distribute works where necessary to maintain and preserve their collections and the use thereof.
- Certain performances and displays are subject to special exemptions, such as the public display of a copy of a copyrighted work, by the owner of such copy, or the performance of musical works by orchestras if admission to the public is free.
- Private copies of software may be made by a licensee for archival or safeguard purposes.
- Special licences are granted in some countries, by governmental agencies, to translate and publish works written in a foreign language which are not available in the local language.
- Works of deceased authors may be published or translated, in some countries, without the heirs' or assignees' authorization, if these works are not otherwise published within a given term after the author's death.

2.17 Infringement and remedies

Copyright is enforced by means of national and international rules on infringement and remedies. Each country enacts and enforces its own rules on infringement and remedies, but these rules must comply with certain minimum international standards, particularly those set out by the Berne Convention and the TRIPs Agreement. The technicalities of the national systems in this area can vary significantly from one country to another; for instance, civil law systems admit the possibility of granting damaged private parties the right to start criminal actions for copyright infringement, while in the U.S. and other countries of the Anglo-American tradition criminal law actions are initiated by state agents or bodies. However, the practical results depend more on the effectiveness of the enforcement mechanisms than on these legal technicalities. In copyright matters, the unpunished violation of legal rights is not only common but massive, throughout the world, but especially in developing countries. This impunity is often the consequence of the very small value of each individual violation, even if such violations are then repeated millions of times, as is the case with copyright violations through photocopying or the Internet. Sometimes, the ineffectiveness of copyright remedies reflects the ineffectiveness of the legal system of which they are a part.

Generally, any violation of the exclusive rights resulting from copyright – including copyright on translations – constitutes an infringement subject to civil and criminal remedies. It is common for copyright laws to list certain specific infringements, such as manufacturing or distributing illegal copies of a copyrighted work, and to include broader provisions imposing sanctions on all the other copyright infringements not specifically described.

Criminal infringements generally are defined more narrowly and precisely than civil violations.

Article 41 of the TRIPs Agreement provides that member countries shall ensure that certain enforcement procedures are available under their law so as to permit effective action against any act of infringement of intellectual property rights – such as copyright – including expeditious remedies to prevent infringements and remedies which constitute a deterrent to further infringement.

Civil procedures are intended to apply remedies such as the payment of damages to the copyright holder and injunctions aimed at preventing or terminating infringements.

Article 44 of the TRIPs Agreement provides that the judicial authorities of member countries shall have the authority to order a party to desist from an infringement, e.g. to prevent the entry into the channels of commerce in their jurisdiction of imported goods that involve the infringement of an intellectual property right. Member countries can impose other types of injunction, not specifically foreseen by Article 44, such as enjoining the continued exploitation of a work or ordering that infringing copies be retired from circulation.

Regarding damages, Article 45 of the TRIPs Agreement provides that the judicial authorities of member countries shall have the authority to order the infringer to pay the right holder damages adequate to compensate for the injury the right holder has suffered because of an infringement of that person's intellectual property right by an infringer who knowingly, or with reasonable grounds to know, engaged in infringing activity. In addition, the judicial authorities shall also have the authority to order the infringer to pay the right holder expenses, which may include appropriate attorney's fees.

Judicial authorities can also order provisional measures, without a full adversarial procedure and even without allowing the defendant to intervene before the measures are decided, to prevent an infringement from occurring, and in particular to prevent infringing goods from entering into the channels of commerce. For example, a copyright owner may request a court to order certain goods to be retained by customs, on the basis of evidence to the effect that the copyright owned by such plaintiff is being infringed by the imported goods; the defendant may only have the right to be heard after the provisional measure has been imposed. Provisional measures may also be imposed to preserve relevant evidence in regard to an alleged infringement.

Criminal penalties may be imposed on copyright infringements, although such penalties are far less common than civil remedies. Article 61 of the TRIPs Agreement provides that member countries shall provide for criminal procedures and penalties to be applied at least in cases of copyright piracy on a commercial scale; in fact, member countries usually provide criminal penalties for most intentional copyright violations implying commercial advantages or economic gain (although they rarely implement such rules). Article 61 also provides:

Remedies available shall include imprisonment and/or monetary fines sufficient to provide a deterrent, consistently with the level of penalties applied for crimes of a corresponding gravity. In appropriate cases, remedies available shall also include the seizure, forfeiture and destruction of the infringing goods and of any materials and implements the predominant use of which has been in the commission of the offence. Members may provide for criminal procedures and penalties to be applied in other cases of infringement of intellectual property rights, in particular where they are committed wilfully and on a commercial scale.

2.18 Neighbouring rights

Neighbouring rights are part of intellectual property and relate to intellectual creations which have economic or spiritual value without qualifying strictly for copyright protection. In particular, they include the rights of performing artists in their performances, the rights of producers of phonograms in their phonograms, and the rights of broadcasting organizations in their radio and television programmes. National laws have also developed neighbouring rights in other intellectual elements, such as the publication of literary works.

Neighbouring rights are not part of the Berne Convention system. They are protected internationally by the Rome Convention, but the number of countries covered by the latter is much smaller – less than one half – than that of members of the Berne Convention. This lack of international coverage created a need to strengthen the effectiveness of international standards for neighbouring rights which was met by including provisions on these rights in the TRIPs Agreement.

Article 14(1) of the TRIPs Agreement requires that member countries grant certain minimum rights to performers, such as the exclusive right to authorize the fixation of their performances – i.e. reducing a work to a material form, such as a record, for subsequent use or reproduction –, the reproduction of such fixations, and the broadcasting or communication to the public of their performances. In this context, performers include actors, singers, musicians, dancers, and other persons who act, sing, deliver, declaim, play in, or otherwise perform literary or artistic works – according to the definition included in Article 3 of the Rome Convention.

Article 14(2) of the TRIPs Agreement provides that producers of phonograms shall enjoy the right to authorize or prohibit the direct or indirect reproduction of their phonograms. Producers of phonograms have been defined – by Article 3 of the Rome Convention – as the persons who, or the legal entities which, are the first to fix the sounds of a performance or other sounds.

With regard to broadcasts, Article 14(3) of the TRIPs Agreement allows member countries to choose between two alternative systems of minimum rights. Member countries may grant the broadcasting organizations exclusive rights to authorize the following acts: fixation, reproduction of fixations, and the rebroadcasting by wireless means of broadcasts, as well as the communication to the public of television broadcasts. Alternatively, member countries may provide owners of copyright in the subject matter of broadcasts with the possibility of preventing those acts in connection with the broadcasts. Broadcasting organizations are defined, by Article 3 of the Rome Convention, as those which transmit sounds or images and sounds by wireless means for public reception.

The TRIPs Agreement also provides the minimum duration of neighbouring rights. Pursuant to its Article 14(5), the term of protection granted to performers and producers of phonograms shall last at least until the end of a period of 50 years computed from the end of the calendar year in which the fixation was made or the performance took place; the protection granted to broadcasting organizations shall last for at least 20 years from the end of the calendar year in which the broadcast took place.

Neighbouring rights are part of the intellectual property system and as such may coexist with copyright over the same subject matter. For example, reproduction of the performance of a translated work requires not only the authorization of the owner of rights in such performance but also of the owner of copyright in the original work and in its translation.

2.19 The international copyright protection system

The nineteenth-century experience showed that, in the absence of an international copyright protection system, individual countries would pursue a self-defeating nationalistic policy, based on the granting of little or no protection to foreign authors, to the immediate benefit of local consumers. This practice resulted in a significant weakening of the copyright system, since any given author is a foreigner in all but one of the countries of the world.

A tendency started in the nineteenth century to overcome this fatal weakness resulting from the fragmentation of the world's legal system into multiple national jurisdictions. Several countries signed to this effect, in 1886, the Berne Convention for the Protection of Literary and Artistic Works, many of whose provisions have been mentioned in the preceding paragraphs. The Berne Convention has been modified several times. Although until recently many important countries, such as the U.S., were not part of this Convention, it nowadays binds most countries of the world. It includes different types of provision for the protection of the rights of authors in their works, namely:

- Establishment of a Union. The member countries constitute a Union for the protection of the rights of authors in their literary and artistic works. Different provisions of the Berne Convention define the operation of this Union.

- National treatment. According to Article 5(1), authors shall enjoy, in respect of works protected by the Convention, in countries of the Union other than the country of origin of the work, the rights which their respective laws grant to their nationals, as well as the rights specially granted by the Convention. Thus, for example, if country X decides to grant certain rental rights to authors, these rights must extend not only to national authors, but also to foreign authors from countries included within the Convention's scope. Article 3 defines who these authors are.
- Non-reciprocity. This principle is not expressly included in the Convention, but follows from the national treatment rule. If country X grants a certain benefit to its authors, it must extend this benefit to the authors of all the other member countries, under the national treatment rule, without the possibility of limiting the rights of foreign authors to what they are in their own countries. There are some exceptions to this basic rule, allowing member countries, in some cases, to weaken the protection granted to foreign authors who are nationals of countries which grant insufficient copyright protection.
- Independence of rights. Each country grants copyright protection to nationals of Berne Convention countries, according to the national law of the country granting such protection, independently from the existence of protection in the country of origin of the work (Article 5(2)).
- No formal requirements. Copyright protection within the limits of the Convention shall not be subject to any formality (Article 5(2)). This is of great practical importance, since it minimizes the cost of copyright protection throughout the world; this protection results from the existence of a copyrightable work.
- Minimum level of protection. The Convention requires that certain economic and moral rights be granted to authors; these rights have been described in the preceding paragraphs of this chapter. The Convention specifies other minimum levels of protection in connection with matters such as the duration of copyright and certain aspects of enforcement.
- Limitations and exceptions. The Convention expressly permits member countries to provide certain limitations and exceptions to copyright protection. These rules have been described in paragraph 2.16.
- Protection greater than that resulting from the Convention. Article 19 of the Convention provides that the provisions of such Convention shall not preclude the making of a claim to the benefit of any greater protection which may be granted by legislation in a member country. For instance, member countries may grant – and do grant – longer terms of protection than those required by the Convention, or may extend economic or moral rights, to the benefit of authors, which do not exist

or are not required by the Convention.
- Special provisions regarding developing countries. The Berne Convention includes a complex set of provisions, intended to improve the position of developing countries in the context of the world copyright system, e.g. allowing special licences for the translation of works in these countries. These provisions have proven to be generally inapplicable or irrelevant.

Although the Berne Convention has had a major influence on the structure and contents of the national copyright laws, it had several severe shortcomings. By requiring the protection of moral rights, which are alien to the Anglo-American legal tradition, it discouraged several countries from participating in this legal area; thus, the U.S. only officially entered the Berne Convention system by means of the Berne Convention Implementation Act of 1988. An alternative international system was sought through the Universal Copyright Convention, of 1952, but this Convention was narrower and practically weaker. Both the Berne Convention and the Universal Copyright Convention had a fatal flaw, namely that member countries could openly violate the provisions of these conventions, without becoming subject to significant enforcement or sanction proceedings. Although both conventions include provisions on dispute resolution, enforcement and sanctions finally depended on the willingness of the infringing country to submit itself to the relevant procedures and sanctions, hardly a recipe for effectiveness.

In the 1980s, an international movement started to strengthen the effective protection granted to intellectual property by means of broadening the scope and enforceability of the international treaties applicable to such property. The basic idea was to tie intellectual property protection to commercial benefits; individual countries would have access to these benefits only if they agreed to a complex package including stronger international rules for intellectual property protection. This movement resulted in the Uruguay Round of negotiations, which in turn generated the World Trade Organization agreements included in the Marrakech Act of 1994. These agreements included one on Trade Related Aspects of Intellectual Property Rights, also known as TRIPs or the TRIPs Agreement. This Agreement applies to intellectual property in general, and includes some specific provisions on copyright and neighbouring rights. The relevant aspects of the TRIPs Agreement may be summarized as follows:

- Member countries of the TRIPs Agreement are under the obligation to enforce the provisions of the Berne Convention, other than those on moral rights. This is of great practical significance since it implies that a violation of the Berne Convention, e.g. by not granting adequate protection to copyright, also becomes a violation of the TRIPs Agreement and this in turn makes applicable the dispute settlement mechanisms and

the sanctions provided by the World Trade Organization system. The result is that copyright owners enjoy the minimum standards set both by the Berne Convention and by TRIPs, enforced – with a few exceptions – through the mechanisms of the World Trade Organization.
- The TRIPs Agreement reiterates the applicability to copyright of the national treatment principle, and extends it to neighbouring rights; each member country shall accord to the nationals of other member countries treatment no less favourable than that it accords to its own nationals with regard to the protection of intellectual property.
- Article 4 of the TRIPs Agreement includes a most-favoured-nation treatment clause. This requires, with regard to the protection of intellectual property, that any advantage, favour, privilege or immunity granted by a member country to the nationals of any other country shall be accorded immediately and unconditionally to the nationals of all other member countries. Thus, if country X agrees to grant certain additional copyright protection to the nationals of country A, it must grant the same additional rights to the nationals of all other member countries.
- Other than requiring member countries to comply with the Berne Convention, the TRIPs Agreement includes few rules on the substantive protection of copyright. It requires that computer programs and data compilations be protected by copyright, and that certain exclusive rights be extended to the rental of computer programs and cinematographic works. It also provides that, with the exception of photographic works or works of applied art, if the term of protection is calculated on a basis other than the life of a natural person, "such term shall be no less than 50 years from the end of the calendar year of authorized publication, or, failing such authorized publication within 50 years from the making of the work, 50 years from the end of the calendar year of making" (Article 12).
- It includes (Article 13) a general provision on limitations and exceptions to copyright protection, of a more general scope than the similar provision included in the Berne Convention: "Members shall confine limitations or exceptions to exclusive rights to certain special cases which do not conflict with a normal exploitation of the work and do not unreasonably prejudice the legitimate interests of the right holder".
- Article 14 of the TRIPs Agreement includes certain minimum standards on neighbouring rights, described in paragraph 2.18, above.
- A major difference with the Berne Convention is that the TRIPs Agreement includes multiple and detailed provisions on the enforcement of intellectual property rights, including minimum standards on civil and administrative procedures and remedies, provisional measures, border measures and criminal procedures.

- The TRIPs Agreement includes special rules on disputes and sanctions. If a member country considers that another country is violating the rules of TRIPs – e.g. by not complying with the required levels of copyright protection – it may file a complaint with the World Trade Organization. This results in a negotiation period; if an agreement is not reached, a special panel issues a report. The panel report may be appealed before the Appellate Body, a permanent organ of the World Trade Organization. If a decision favourable to the complaining country is reached, such country may impose trade sanctions on the infringing member, within the limits derived from such decision.

The dispute settlement procedures provided by TRIPs are only available to member countries. If a national of a member country considers that another country does not comply with TRIPs' standards, it must request its own country to intervene on its behalf before the World Trade Organization.

CASE STUDIES

A. NN, a translator, finds that copies of one of her translations are being manufactured and distributed without her authorization in Ruritania, a member of the Berne Convention and of TRIPs. Ruritania's copyright laws include provisions prohibiting these acts of manufacturing and distribution, but enforcement of these provisions – as is the case with many other aspects of Ruritanian law – is weak and ineffective. NN wishes to know if she can resort to TRIPs' or other procedures to force Ruritania into effectively protecting her rights.

Comments: Although TRIPs includes rules on enforcement, procedures and remedies, its provisions are generally applied with regard to the rules on these matters included in each member country's laws, and not with respect to the actual enforcement of such rules. Thus, if Ruritanian law includes provisions which comply with TRIPs requirements, this will normally be considered as sufficient for Ruritania to comply with TRIPs in this area. In addition, NN cannot resort personally and directly to the World Trade Authorization procedures, but must rather request her own country to start procedures against Ruritania; the decision to do so will normally depend not only from legal considerations but also from political and strategic reasons, e.g. whether this may lead Ruritania to bring actions against NN's home country for other violations.

B. XX has created a computer program which permits a faster and more precise spelling check in various languages. YY creates a program having similar effects but with a different software structure. YY wishes to determine whether he is violating XX's copyright.

Comments: Copyright does not protect the functional aspects of intellectual works but rather the expression of the work. Thus, the functional equivalence of XX's and YY's programs does not imply that there is an infringement of XX's copyright and in fact may work against XX's intention to file copyright actions against YY. The functional aspects of software or of other technologies are protected by other types of intellectual property, such as patents; however, only some countries extend patent protection to software.

C. MM, a national of a Berne Convention country, has translated a classical work from Latin into English. While trying to determine what protection she has worldwide on her translation, she comes across the copyright statutes of A, a South American country, which provides that no copyright action is allowed in favour of an author until the relevant work is filed with the local authority. A is also a member of the Berne Convention. MM wishes to know the copyright status of her translation in country A.

Comments: National laws apply different rules to determine the consequences of a contradiction between domestic statutes and international treaties effective in the relevant countries. Some systems provide that international treaties are immediately effective and that they overrule inconsistent local rules; under these systems, MM would be able to directly enforce her rights in country A, without registration, since the Berne Convention's rules would prevail over the local filing requirements. Other systems only consider international treaties as enforceable if they are incorporated into the domestic legal system by an express enactment.

D. Doña Petrona, a famous cook, publishes a book in Spanish, including her favourite recipes. Smith, a restaurant owner, uses some of these recipes in his restaurant. Dos Santos, a Brazilian publisher, includes the translation into Portuguese of several of these recipes, as literally described by Doña Petrona, in a book featuring a selection of famous recipes. Do Smith and Dos Santos violate Doña Petrona's copyright?

Comments: Doña Petrona has copyright in the expression she has used, i.e. the verbal description of certain recipes. She does not have copyright on ideas, in this case the recipes themselves. Smith and anyone else are thus free to put these recipes into practice, and even to describe them with different words. But Dos Santos has reproduced Doña Petrona's expression of the recipes, although in a different language, and has therefore breached Doña Petrona's copyright.

3. The Copyright Protection of Translations

3.1 Basic rules of copyright protection as applied to translations

Copyright law has developed specific and relatively detailed rules regarding translations. Although the rights of translators are also governed and protected by other types of rules, to be discussed in the following chapters, copyright law addresses the specific issues posed by translations and includes special rules dealing with such issues.

Translations are universally considered as intellectual works protected by copyright. Article 2(3) of the Berne Convention expressly requires member countries to grant such protection. National statutes generally include translations among the types of work protected by copyright. However, even if translations are not listed among the types of work protected by copyright, they are protected by national laws under the general provisions which extend copyright to intellectual or literary works.

The present status of translations as intellectual works protected by copyright has not always been accepted. Intellectual works protected by copyright require a certain level of individual creativity, and it may be argued that translations may be purely mechanical or that they do not allow the translator scope for his or her creativity.

Although this argument still has some impact on the determination of the limits of copyright protection for translations, it has been largely rejected by contemporary treaties and national statutes, which generally include translations as intellectual works protected by copyright. Even in the absence of such provisions, case law has decided that translations are protected by copyright.[1]

Contemporary copyright law generally classifies translations as derivative works. Some statutes, such as the U.S. Copyright Act (section 106(2)), expressly follow this approach. In other legal systems, this characteristic is generally accepted even if it is not expressed in the relevant statutes. It implies that the intellectual content of the translated work is included in the translation. A reproduction of the translation therefore also implies, from a copyright law perspective, a reproduction of the translated work. Some legal systems reach similar results by using a different terminology. For example, German law considers that translations are "adaptations" (*Bearbeitungen*, in Article 3 of the German Copyright Law); English law also uses wording based on "adaptation" (see Bently 1993:505). However, it should be borne in mind that in other legal

---

[1] See, under English law, Millar v. Taylor, 98 Eng. Rep. 203 (K.B. 1769) ("translations … in respect of the property, may be considered as new works").

systems the word "adaptation" and its equivalents in the relevant language do not extend to translations.

The status of translations as derivative works has several legal consequences. First, copyright in the translations does not limit or prevent the existence and effects of copyright in the original or translated work; this principle is frequently expressly included in national statutes and results from Article 2(3) of the Berne Convention. A consequence of this principle is that the owner of copyright over the translated work can exercise his or her economic and moral rights in connection with translations of such work. Hence, for example, a translation of a work protected by copyright may not be reproduced without the authorization of the owner of the copyright in the translated work; this prohibition extends to the translator and to third parties. However, the fact that there are separate rights over the derivative work – the translation – has several implications with regard to the actual content of the rights of the copyright owner of the translated work, as will be discussed in this chapter.

Second, the owner of copyright in the translation may not reproduce or otherwise exploit such translation without the authorization of the owner of copyright in the translated work. The reproduction and other types of use or exploitation of the translation also imply, legally, a similar reproduction, use or exploitation of the translated work, and this is only possible with the authorization of the owner of such translated work.

Third, copyright in the translation is separate from copyright in the original or translated work. Copyright in the translation belongs, at least initially, to the author of such translation. The owner of copyright in the original or translated work is not allowed to reproduce or otherwise exploit a translation without the authorization of the owner of copyright in such translation. However, the owner of copyright in the original or translated work may authorize other translations, and these are intellectual works different from the initial translation, which may be reproduced or otherwise exploited without the consent of the owner of copyright in the initial translation.

One basic result of these characteristics of translations as derivative works is that reproduction and other forms of exploitation of a translation are only possible with the consent of both the owner of copyright in the original work and of the owner of copyright in the translation. They can reciprocally block each other's reproduction or exploitation of the translation. Since such blocking deprives both parties of the economic benefits derived from the translation, they have an incentive to negotiate and reach an agreement as to how the translation shall be reproduced or otherwise exploited. In fact, translations normally take place on the basis of a preexisting agreement to that effect.

3.2 The legal concept of translation

Whether a text constitutes a translation or not is a question whose answer has significant legal effects. A translation is a derivative work, subject to the general copyright rules applicable to derivative works and to the specific copyright rules applicable to translations. A text which does not constitute a translation is not subject to these rules.

There is no generally accepted legal definition of translation. The World Intellectual Property Organization (1988:215) defines translation as "the expression of a work in a language other than that of the original version". This definition, although useful, shows that the limits of the legal concept of translation are far from clear, and that such concept has significant anomalies from the perspective of basic copyright principles.

One of the most basic and universal rules of intellectual property is that copyright does not protect ideas, but rather the expression of ideas. However, the fact that the rights of the owner of copyright in the original work extend to translated versions of such work implies that different expressions – or, at least, expressions in different languages – of the same concepts are considered to be protected by copyright in the original expression or in the original language. Thus, in the context of the copyright regime of translations, copyright extends to a certain conceptual framework, regardless of the language it is expressed in.

There are several reasons which may justify this perceived anomaly. The traditional idea/expression dichotomy – expression being protected by copyright, and ideas being beyond such protection – is not rigid, and the case of translations is just an example of its flexibility. Changing the names of the characters in a play implies changing the expression of such play, and yet it will not be enough to place the play, with the names changed, beyond the reach of copyright in the original play. "Expression", in the area of copyright, does not necessarily mean a univocal succession of words or signs, but rather has a more abstract reach.

Also, from an economic point of view, most of the value of a translated work is derived from the original work. Although there are exceptions to this rule, it can be empirically proved with the evidence resulting from the contractual negotiations between owners of copyright in the original work and translators. The owners of copyright in the original work normally face a market for translations – i.e. there are several available translators for each given work – with a corresponding market price, which is normally lower than the price of the original work. The market value of the original work would disappear in the markets for works in other languages if copyright in the original work did not extend to such other languages. The extension of copyright in the original work to translations permits a market remuneration for translators and the international effectiveness of copyright, which is one of the underlying goals of the contemporary copyright regime.

Once it is admitted that copyright in the original work extends to such work's expression in different languages, it becomes necessary to determine the standards to be used to decide that a text in a given target or receiving language is the translation of a text in the original language. A frequently applied standard is that of meaning; a target language text is a translation of a text in the original language if it has the same meaning as the original text. This standard may be enough for legal purposes but it creates – as is common with all legal concepts – major difficulties and uncertainties. The concept of "meaning" is famously difficult from a philosophical point of view.[2] In addition, each language has its own nuances and conceptual frameworks which frequently cannot be reflected by other languages; in this context, "meaning" becomes distorted as a text is expressed in a different language. Also, translation – as is especially the case in poetry – may imply or require a certain level of creativity. The legal issue, in these cases, is to determine when creativity reaches such a level that a purported translation becomes an original text. One may remember Chesterton's comments (2011:269) about Fitzgerald's celebrated "translation" of Omar Khayyam's *Rubayats*:

> Edward Fitzgerald, a cultured eccentric ... produced what professed to be a translation of the Persian poet Omar, who wrote quatrains about wine and roses and things in general. Whether the Persian original, in its own Persian way, was greater or less than this version I must not discuss here, and could not discuss anywhere. But it is quite clear that Fitzgerald's work is much too good to be a good translation. It is as personal and creative a thing as ever was written.

The Spanish language versions of the *Rubayats* certainly differ significantly from Fitzgerald's.

On this basis, the identity of meaning between texts in different language is a relatively vague standard whose enforcement requires a fair degree of personal judgement by the court or authority deciding whether a text is a translation.

Another dimension in the legal definition of translation and its use in specific cases has to do with the concept of language. In most translations, a given text in a clearly identified language results in a translated text, also in a clearly identified language, e.g. from French into English. Some cases are more dubious. Languages tend to have regional or historical variations. Sixteenth-century English or Spanish differ significantly from contemporary English or Spanish. This leads to the query of whether a contemporary version of a text written in a historical version of a given language constitutes a translation or an adaptation. The answer has legal implications, since translations and adaptations are not governed by the same rules; e.g. some countries provide special exceptions in favour of translations of works protected by copyright, which do not extend to adaptations. The solution, as with so many legal issues, is a matter of degree and judicial judgement. Seamus Heaney's

---

[2] Bellos (2011:69) reminds us that "meaning is no simple thing".

celebrated modern English version of *Beowulf* is marketed as a translation and should legally be considered to constitute a translation and not an adaptation. But children's adaptations of Dickens, for instance, are marketed as adaptations and not as translations, and this usage should also be considered as legally valid. One possible test would be whether readers in the target language understand the original. However, as will be examined in the next paragraph, this test is not applied in other circumstances, and does not have significant legal support. It is difficult to apply, because historical or geographical variations of a language may have words or passages beyond the reach of some readers, the rest of such variations being sufficiently clear. This would require some kind of quantitative test determining what degree of difficulty is sufficient for a version to qualify as a translation; no such test is generally accepted in comparative law. For example, the classic Argentine poem, *Martín Fierro*, is written in a now extinct variety of Spanish spoken in rural areas of Argentina, but it can be read by modern Argentine readers with the help of a relatively small glossary, normally attached to contemporary editions. How large does the glossary need to be for a judge to determine that an adapted version is no longer an adaptation but rather a translation? Does a version for Spanish or Mexican readers – which would require a broader adaptation or a larger glossary – imply a translation? There are no clear-cut answers or tests applicable to these questions.

Also related to the idea of language is the applicability of the concept of translation between two idioms normally recognized as languages but which are comprehensible for readers of the other language. Thus, for example, Spanish is frequently understood by Portuguese readers, and Galician – nowadays a language recognized and protected under the Spanish constitution – even more so, being closer to Portuguese than to Spanish. However, a test based on whether a language is understandable by readers of a different language is not legally applied to distinguish translations from adaptations. Also, a test based on the degree of effort required to create the target language text would be inapplicable, in accordance with the general rules applied to determine whether an intellectual creation qualifies for copyright protection, which tend to exclude standards based on effort or "sweat of the brow". A relatively easy translation from Portuguese into Spanish is as much a translation, from a legal point of view, as a translation from Chinese into Basque. The applicable test is not one based on difficulty but rather on the choices and creativity required from the translator.

For a translation to qualify as such for copyright purposes, it is not necessary for the original or the target language to legally qualify as languages or official languages. In fact, many countries do not have a legal concept of language or of national language, but this is no obstacle for the copyright protection of translations. Either the original or the target language may be dead languages, regional dialects, slang or oral languages.[3] Translations between mathematical languages would legally qualify as translations; authorities are divided, however, as to whether translation from one computer language into another, both of them not to be used by human readers, legally qualify as translation from a copyright point of view.

A major difficulty upon drawing the legal limits of translation is posed by the need to define the verbal units whose translation may be protected. Translating a word, or a commonly used sentence, does not create copyright on the translation. But short passages, such as sentences included on tombstones or in comic books, have been considered to be legally subject to copyrightable translations. The test applicable in these cases must be based on the general theory which supports the protection of translation by copyright. Translations require a level of choice between different alternatives – in the target language –, verbal creativity and individual variation which is deemed sufficient by international treaties and national statutes to protect them as intellectual creations. But if there is no individual input – as in the translation of well-known individual words – a translation does not imply intellectual creation – in the legal sense of the expression – and is not protected by copyright.

Use of the common copyright standards on creativity implies that certain types of translation are far more likely than others to qualify as copyrightable works. Translation of poems, novels and other artistic literary works normally imply a higher level of creativity than translations of legal documents, technical handbooks or forms. However, there is no statutory or conceptual exception against the copyrightable character of translations of specific types of works. Simply stated, some types of translated works are more likely than others to meet the standard of creativity required to achieve copyright protection.

Poor or mistaken translations still qualify legally as such. The poor quality of a translation may impair its economic or intellectual value, but not its copyright protection. However, if a translation is so poor that the identity of meaning is generally lost, it would no longer qualify as a translation, but could still be viewed as an adaptation of the mistranslated original.

In addition, if a purported translation does not provide, in a different language, the expressive content of the original, that is, the meaning of the words that constitute such original, but rather reformulates in a different language the ideas used in the original, it would not qualify as a translation for copyright law purposes. The idea/expression dichotomy, characteristic of copyright law, is applicable in these cases. In the context of translation, as in other intellectual property areas, the copyright rules on translation protect the author's expression, and not his or her ideas thus expressed.

If a text in language A is written by translating from a translation into language B a text originally written in language C, the text in language A would

---

[3] E.g. under German law see Dreier and Schulze (2006:115).

still legally qualify as a translation of the original in language C. This situation is common in Romance languages, where a "difficult" translation – e.g. from German or Chinese – is first undertaken into one language –typically French – and from that language into the other Romance languages. Theoretically, the translation into C is a translation from both the original and from language B, and the copyright owners of both the original and the translation into language B would have rights, including the right of translation to be discussed in 3.3, regarding the translation into language C. However, it may be difficult to prove that a translation has been made in the indirect way described above. In addition, some countries do not extend to translations of translations the same rules applicable to direct translations (see Bently 1993:509).

Translations may be oral or in writing, and may be of written or oral works. However, in countries which apply the fixation requirement for copyright protection – particularly the U.S. under Section 102(a) of the Copyright Act – copyright protection may be limited to works which are fixed in a tangible medium of expression, and copyright may not extend to unrecorded oral translations.

Lack of copyright protection for the original work does not exclude the copyright protection of the translation. Classic works in dead languages, which are in the public domain, may be translated, and the translation will be protected by copyright if it satisfies the usual standards for copyright protection. The fact that there is no copyright on the original work means that certain common limitations bearing on the rights of the translator would be inapplicable in this situation; in particular, the translator needs no authorization to make and publish the translation, and the right of translation, to be discussed in 3.3, is inapplicable in these cases. But the fact that a person is the first to translate a work in the public domain gives such person no exclusive right on the possibility of translating such work, and other persons may generate and publish different translations, also protected by copyright, provided such translations are not copied from the first one and meet the standard requirements of creativity required for copyrightable works.

3.3 The right of translation

Translating a work protected by copyright requires the authorization of the person holding the copyright in such work. This is a general rule in comparative law, imposed by Article 8 of the Berne Convention; this article requires that authors of literary and artistic works have the exclusive right of making and of authorizing the translation of their works throughout the term of protection of their rights in their original work. Provisions complying with Article 8 of the Berne Convention are generally found in national laws; e.g. in Section 106(2) of the U.S. Copyright Act and in Article 23 of the German Copyright Law.

The right of translation is considered to be part of a broader category, namely the right of adaptation. In some legal systems, the relevant statutes do not provide an explicit right of translation, but they do provide a right of adaptation, and this is considered to extend to translations. The relation between these legal categories implies that provisions and transactions related to adaptation rights may include the right of translation, even if no express mention is made of the latter. Thus, an agreement assigning the right of adaptation may be construed as also assigning the right of translation, unless the wording or circumstances of that agreement lead to a different result.

The right of translation is considered to be an exploitation right and not a moral right; these categories have been described in 2.13 and 2.14 above. This characteristic has important legal consequences, given the limitations bearing on the assignment or waiver of moral rights, which therefore do not extend to the right of translation. However, a person who has received the right to translate a given work, and who therefore is allowed to translate it, has to respect the moral rights of such work's author. Hence, the authorized translator may not distort or modify the work in a way which is detrimental to the author's honour or reputation.

The distinction between the right of translation, as an exploitation right, and the moral rights in the original also implies that the acquisition of the right of translation or an authorization pursuant to that right does not free the person acquiring the right or receiving the authorization from the effects of the moral rights on the original. In fact, such moral rights may belong to a person completely different from the assignor or licensor of the right of translation, since moral rights necessarily belong to the author, while the rights of translation may be subject to assignments or other transfers.

Given the contents of moral rights, described in 2.14 above, translations, even if adequately authorized under the right of translation, may conflict with such moral rights in several ways. They may affect the right of integrity by altering the contents of the translated work. A translation modifies the expression of a work but is not in itself an alteration of the work; it may be a violation of moral rights in that work if the translation is so deficient or incomplete as to alter the content or significantly diminish the quality of the original. The right of attribution may be violated if the translation does not properly identify the identity of the translated work and its author. The right of divulgation implies, in this context, that a translation may only be published if the original has been published with the author's authorization; the right of divulgation generally does not extend to each new translated version of the original. The right to withdraw a work, in the countries in which it is applicable, would also extend to translations. The right to modify the work would extend to the translated versions of the work, but would not imply an obligation by the translator to modify the translated work accordingly; rather, in this context it means that the author may generate translations of the work modified in accordance with the moral right to modify the work, and under some legal systems this may require compensation to the owner of the right of translation in the work in its original version.

Another legal consequence of the status of the right of translation as an exploitation right is that the assignment of exploitation rights in general, or the authorization to engage in conduct generally included under such exploitation rights, will normally extend to the right of translation, unless the relevant transaction provides otherwise. Since the wording or context of certain transactions may create doubts regarding whether the right of translation has been included or not within the exploitation rights which are the subject matter of such transactions, it is advisable and common to include express provisions indicating the extent to which translations and the exploitation thereof are included in a specific contract or transaction.

The right of translation normally extends to public uses or reproduction of a translation and not to translations made privately for the translator's use.[4] However, some legal systems do not include this limitation in their statutory provisions and may have no general exception in their copyright laws for private or fair uses. Nevertheless, even under such systems a translation kept exclusively within the translator's reach and use will generally not be considered to be a violation of the right of translation, and it will be considered excusable either as a form of fair use or as a type of private use not reached by copyright and the right of translation.

The right of translation, and the authorizations, licences or assignments granted by the owner of such right, encompass several different elements which are not always clearly distinguished in contracts and other transactions related to translations. A first element is the right to make the translation; as discussed in the preceding paragraph this right may generally exist without prior authorization from the owner of copyright in the original, to the extent that the translation remains private and falls within the exceptions in favour of fair or private use. A second element is the right to publish the translation; this requires the authorization of the owner of copyright in the original. Such authorization is also necessary for the right to reproduce the translation. Finally, the right of translation also extends to the other economic and exploitation rights described in 2.13 above; the acts of exploitation falling within the scope of these rights, regarding a translation, may only take place with the authorization of the owner of the right of translation in the original work. Hence, for example, if X reproduces a translation made by Y of an original work whose copyright is owned by Z, X is violating Z's copyright, including Z's right of translation.

The complexity of the right of translation bears on the drafting and effects of transactions related to such right. The simple authorization to translate a text could be construed as not extending beyond its literal meaning, and hence

---

[4] Under German law, see Dreier and Schulze (2006:325).

not implying the authorization to reproduce, publish or otherwise exploit the resulting translation. If such approach is followed, the right to translate given to the person receiving the authorization would be devoid of economic value. Generally, contracts and other transactions which authorize translations define in more detail the rights given to the person authorized to translate. They include clauses indicating what rights of publication and distribution such person shall have, the duration of such rights and other limits applicable to the use and exploitation of the translation. Even in the absence of express provisions such as these, the right to reproduce, publish or otherwise exploit the translation may be inferred from other elements of the transaction involved. The fact that a substantial consideration has been paid for the translation rights will lead to the inference that the person paying for such rights intended to publish or economically exploit the translation. But the context of these transactions and of the negotiations preceding them may also operate as elements restricting the scope of the translation rights. For example, if an Italian publisher is authorized to translate a work, and to publish and distribute it, both parties would have normally acted in the expectation that only an Italian translation is foreseen, and that no translation rights for other languages are included, unless this additional extension is expressly mentioned by the parties.

If a person translates a work without proper authorization, and then reproduces or publishes such translation, there will normally be a violation of the right of translation in the original work as well as a violation of the reproduction right inherent in the copyright in the original work; reproduction of the translation also implies reproduction of the intellectual work which has been translated. This generally has no impact on the amount of damages or other sanctions imposed, but may have legal significance in cases in which it is not clear whether a translation has taken place, particularly when different versions of a computer program are involved. It becomes unnecessary to determine whether a translation has taken place or not, if a copyright violation clearly results from a reproduction, in a different computer language, of the original version of the program.[5]

A much debated issue in comparative law is whether a translation obtains copyright protection if it has been made in violation of the right of translation in the original. Several arguments have been advanced and used to deny such protection: that it would create an economic incentive for copyright violations; that a copyright infringer should not profit from the infringement; that legal protection should not be extended to illegal conduct or the consequences thereof.

The U.S. Copyright Act denies copyright protection to infringing translations. Leaffer (1995:47) summarizes the law in this area as follows:

---

[5] See for example, under Canadian law, Apple Computer v. Mackintosh Computers Ltd. (1988), 44 DLR (4h) 74.

> A derivative work copyright can only be obtained when the author legally used the material on which the derivative work was based. Section 103(a) of the Copyright Act states that no copyright can be claimed for any part of a derivative or collective work that has used the pre-existing material unlawfully. This prevents an unlawful user of the underlying work from profiting from unlawful use, and protects aspects of the work that were unlawfully derived from pre-existing material. ... Thus, an unauthorized translation of a novel could not be copyrighted at all.

However, the prevailing contemporary view, in comparative law, is that copyright in the translation – initially held by the translator – extends to translations which infringe the right of translation in the original.[6] A key element in this line of thought is that copyright in the infringing translation does not imply the right to use or otherwise exploit such translation; no such right exists, by hypothesis, because there is a violation of rights in the original. Copyright in the infringing translation only means that the owner of such copyright may prevent other parties from using or otherwise exploiting such translation; the owner of this copyright has the right to prohibit the use of the infringing translation, but such right does not imply that its owner may use or exploit the infringing translation. Copyright in the infringing translation creates an obstacle for third parties wishing to use or exploit such translation. In addition, copyright law already provides specific sanctions for copyright violations; these violations do not imply that the infringer or the infringer's conduct falls completely beyond the reach of protection by the legal system, but rather that the infringer is subject to specific sanctions – damages, fines, etc. – provided by the applicable laws. It would not be legally correct, on this basis, to impose additional sanctions on the infringing translator, when the law already establishes what the sanctions should be.

3.4 Ownership of copyright in translations

The general rules on copyright ownership, described in 2.8 above, are applicable to ownership of copyright in translation. The fact that translations are derivative works has multiple effects on the consequences of such rules on translations.

A translation protected by copyright implies that two sets of rights bear on that intellectual work: copyright in the original and copyright regarding the translation. Copyright in the original extends to copies and other acts of exploitation of the translation. The translation embodies the translated work

---

[6] See for example, under German law, Dreier and Schulze (2006:123); under Argentine law, Emery (1999:155).

and therefore it may not be reproduced or otherwise exploited without the authorization of the owner of copyright in the translated work. Also, the publication or any other conduct related to the translation must respect the moral rights in the original.

A separate set of rights extends to the translation. It may not be reproduced or otherwise exploited without the authorization of the owner of copyright in the translation. These limitations extend also to the author or copyright owner of the original; he or she may not reproduce or exploit the translation without the authorization of the owner of copyright in the translation. The author of the translation, in addition, has moral rights in the translation.

Copyright in the translation exists even if the original is no longer protected by copyright. A new translation of the *Odyssey* into English is copyrightable although there is no copyright in the original. Reproduction of that translation would only require the authorization of the copyright owner of the translation.

Copyright ownership in a translation only extends to that specific translation. It does not extend to other translations which do not involve plagiarism of the original. The owner of the right of translation – described in 3.3 above – may authorize new translations of the original, in the same or other languages, unless he or she has granted exclusive rights to a given translator. These new translations will have separate copyright owned originally by the authors of each different translation.

A translation is not necessarily a collective, joint or composite work (these categories were described in 2.9 above). From a copyright perspective, a translation is a derivative work, with authors who are separate from those who created the original and with economic and moral rights belonging exclusively to such authors, or to their heirs or assignees. It is not considered to be a joint effort between the translator and the original's author. The original's author creates a given copyrightable work, and the translator creates a separate work – which has to meet the standards of copyright protection – protected by a different set of rights. However, translations, such as other works, may be collective, joint or composite works, if they have the characteristics of these copyright categories. A translation may be a joint work, in which separate translators participate without separating or distinguishing their individual participation. It may be a collective work, if their creative contributions are separate and identifiable, for example, translations of different entries in an encyclopaedia. It may also be a composite work, as in the case of a play created by translating different poems and literary works from a foreign language. If a translation qualifies as a joint, collective or composite work, rights in that translation will be governed by the general copyright rules on these types of work, described in 2.9 above.

An issue with increasing significance in connection with translations is that related to the status of translations generated by or with the assistance of computers. This is a general problem of copyright law, but it is especially important in the area of translation due to the increasing use of computers and to the improved quality of the translations they generate.

To analyse this issue, certain basic premises are necessary. There is no general prohibition against the copyright protection of intellectual works generated by or with the assistance of computers. Although intellectual works protected by copyright require the existence of an individual who acts as author, it is possible to identify such individual in the case of works generated by computers, in the form of the person who operates the computer or of the computer programmer, among other possibilities.

A second premise is that copyrightable work must have an element of creativity or originality, as has been described in 2.3 above. The mere effort or cost – as is involved in computer-generated works – is not enough, although the level of creativity is not required to be high. One test applied to determine whether this requirement is satisfied is whether the author has used his or her liberty to choose among several possible expressions.[7]

On the basis of these premises, the extension to translations of the general copyright rules applicable to authorship and creativity requires a basic distinction between computer-assisted and computer-generated works.

Computer-assisted works imply the existence of creative activities, by one or more individuals, not performed with the direct intervention of a computer; the computer provides certain elements which are used by these individuals to create the work. For example, an individual translator may use a computer to obtain electronic translations of individual words or short phrases, so as to speed up the translation process, which is performed by the individual using the translated elements. The final work, or the final stages of such work, have an identifiable individual author.

Computer-generated works are the result of the operation of a computer. This operation, in turn, is the consequence of instructions directly or indirectly issued by individuals, and of the operation of one or more computer programs, which have one or more authors. Whatever individual creative elements exist in these computer-generated works, they are located at the initial stages of the creation of such works, that is at the level of setting up a computer program or of operating the computer. If the individual creative element is placed after the computer has finished its operations, the result would be a computer-assisted work.

Copyright in computer-assisted works belongs to the individual or individuals who perform the creative activities on the elements produced by the computer. However, if the operation of the computer has a creative component – particularly, choice by the computer operator between different alternatives provided by the computer – there will be a joint work attributable to the

---

[7] See, under Swiss law, Dessemontet (1999:123).

computer operator and to the individual or individuals who perform creative activities on the elements produced by the computer. In this context, the function of the computer is not radically different from that of a dictionary used for purposes of a translation; the dictionary's author is not a joint author of the translation, but if a person actively selects words from the dictionary, in collaboration with the person "writing" the translation, this selection process may create an element of joint authorship.

In the case of computer-generated works, several alternatives are possible, though only some of them are relevant in comparative law. One is to consider that the fact that the translation is computer-generated implies that it lacks creativity, and that therefore it is not subject to copyright protection. This approach is generally not used. The fact that a translation is computer-generated may indicate, under some circumstances and in specific cases, that it has no creative element, but does not necessarily deny the existence of such element or of copyright protection. The computer-generated translation is not a work protected by copyright if it is limited to the repetition of preexisting translations, or to the mechanical assembly of preexisting translations or otherwise lacks originality or creativity.[8] But the fact that the translation has been generated by a computer does not negate copyright protection if the translation satisfies the originality and creativity requirements, due to the participation of individuals at any of the possible levels of development of a computer-generated work, particularly the design of the applicable program, the operation of such program or the subsequent elaboration of the computer-generated materials.

Another possibility in determining authorship of computer-generated works is to attribute authorship to the author of the program used to generate such works. The logic behind this approach is that a program constitutes a set of electronic instructions, operating on a machine, so that the author of the program may be seen as generating the translation indirectly, with a machine's participation, as is the case with many other types of intellectual work. The difficulty with this approach is that the author of the program does not create or envision a specific translation but simply creates the mechanism which another person sets in motion so as to produce specific translations. As stated in the context of U.S. law (Leaffer 1995:80):

> The programmer did not himself fix the work. He created the possibility of a work, but did not embody it in the tangible medium of expression. The user is the one who did that, and copyright law confers authorship on the person who fixes the work.

Generally, if the computer-generated work has the elements of originality and creativity necessary for copyright protection, the operator of the computer will

---

[8] See, under German law, Dreier and Schulze (2006:115.0).

be considered to be the author of such work. As in other types of work, the computer operator must have exercised some degree of choice between different possibilities opened by the computer instruments used, or of manipulation of such instruments (ibid):

> One who simply turns on a computer and inserts a program ... would be hard put to claim originality. There must be some evidence of choice, selection or intellectual labor constituting originality. The range of user originality is quite easy to find in the output generated through use of a word processing program, but at the other end of the continuum, for computer-generated works involving insignificant or no user discretion, copyright should be denied.

Special rules apply to copyright in translations in the case of works made for hire. These special rules are the result of extending to translations the general rules on copyright in works made for hire, described in 2.10 above.

Copyright, in the case of translations made for hire, belongs to the employer or to the person who has hired the translator. This basic rule has multiple variations when applied to specific situations related to translations.

A first difficulty involves determining whether a given translation is within the scope of the work for which the translation has been hired. If the work to be translated is expressly identified, it will fall under the rules applicable to works made for hire. In many cases, however, a translator is employed to perform translations which are ordered by the employer during the course of the employment, without identifying such translators individually. In such cases, it is necessary to establish whether a given translation is part of the translator's employment relationship, particularly in cases in which the employer does not determine case by case the translations to be undertaken by the hired translator. Various rules are used by the different national laws to solve this type of issue. In some cases, the determining factor is whether the employer controls the manner and means of the translation; in other systems, the fact that the translator has used the intellectual or other resources of the employer may be determinant. Generally, if the translation is undertaken pursuant to instructions or requests of the employer, it will be considered to fall within the scope of the employment relationship, even if performed outside normal working hours, although this last fact may have an impact on the payments due to the translators, depending on the applicable employment laws.

In the case of works made for hire, based on a contract to that effect between the translator and the person ordering the work, the agreement will determine the scope of the works governed by its provisions. These agreements may refer to specific translations of identified works – in which case they will normally not be construed as extending to other works – or may encompass a certain category of works, such as those a translator is requested to translate during a given period. In these cases copyright will not pass to the person paying for the translation with regard to translations which do not fall within the limits provided by the agreement under which the translator was hired.

A second issue regarding which different legal systems provide varying solutions is that of the original copyright owner. In civil law systems, the principle that the original author and copyright owner is always the individual creator of the intellectual work applies even in the case of works made for hire; the special rules applicable to works made for hire imply that this original copyright is automatically transferred to the employer or to the person commissioning the work. In Anglo-American legal systems, the employer or the person who commissioned the work is the original owner of the copyright; Section 201(b) of the U.S. Copyright Act is an example of this approach. In most cases, there are no practical differences between the effects of these different basic rules. However, under some circumstances, the differences as to the identity of the original copyright owner may have practical consequences. In particular, under systems such as the U.S.'s, the employer or the person commissioning the work owns the entire copyright, unless there are express contractual agreements between the parties extending the author's rights. In civil law systems, copyright is transferred to the employer or to the person commissioning the work only to the extent provided by the statutory rules on works made for hire or by the contract pursuant to which the translation is made.

A third type of issue relates to moral rights. These rights, described in 2.14 above, apply to translations and to works made for hire. Civil law systems follow a highly protective approach towards the author's moral rights. These rights belong to the translator even in the case of works made for hire, and in civil law systems they may not be waived or transferred to the employer or to the person owning the economic or exploitation rights in the translation. In the Anglo-American legal sphere, although moral rights are applicable, as required by the Berne Convention, the possibility of waiving or transferring such rights is much broader than in civil law systems.

3.5 The legal content of copyright in translation

Copyright in translation is based on the distinction between the translated work and the translation as derivative work. The translation and copyright therein do not affect the copyright status of the translated work. The owner of copyright in the translated work may exercise all of his or her rights regarding such work, as they existed before the translation took place. These rights extend to the translation, which is viewed as a variation or adaptation of the original work. Therefore, the translator and the owner of copyright in the translation may not reproduce it or otherwise exploit it without the authorization of the copyright owner of the original work.

Copyright in the translation should be distinguished from the right to translate and from the right to reproduce or otherwise exploit the translation. The owner of copyright in the original has a right of translation, described in 3.3 above. This right would be violated by a translator who translates the work without proper authorization by the copyright owner in the original, but does not give such copyright owner an intellectual property right in the translation. As discussed in 3.3, some legal systems may deny copyright in favour of the infringing translator, but do not grant copyright in the translation to the owner of copyright in the original. But even if the translation has been properly authorized by the owner of copyright in the original, this does not necessarily imply the right of the translator to reproduce or to otherwise exploit the translation. These rights are different from the right to translate, and though they may be implied from the authorization to translate – as has been analysed in 3.3 – they may also be excluded from such authorization.

The authorization to translate does not prevent the owner of copyright in the original work from making his or her own translations, or from authorizing other translations in the same or different languages. These rights are retained by such owner unless they are part of a contractual arrangement to the contrary, particularly an agreement to the effect that only the authorized translator will have the right to translate the original work into certain languages or into any language. Additional translations in the same language are protected as separate derivative works, provided they comply with the novelty and creativity standards applicable to all copyrightable works. If they do not comply with such standards, the apparently new translations may be regarded as illegal reproductions of the initial translation.

The author of the translation is the original owner of copyright in that translation. The elements of such copyright are those which are characteristic of copyright in general; they include the economic and moral rights described in 2.13 and 2.14 above. Therefore, for example, no unauthorized party may reproduce the translation or affect its integrity without permission from the owner of copyright in that translation. These rights may be exercised even against the owner of copyright in the original.

The owner of copyright in the translation does not necessarily have the right to publish, reproduce or otherwise exploit such translation. He or she has the right to prevent the reproduction or exploitation of the translation by other persons, but not necessarily the right to reproduce it or exploit it by himself or herself. The reason for this rule is that the reproduction or exploitation of the translation also implies the reproduction or exploitation of the original work, and such reproduction or exploitation is only possible with the consent of the owner of the copyright in the original work. The reproduction or exploitation of a translation requires the consent of both the owner of copyright in the original work and of the owner of the copyright in the translation.

A third party wishing to reproduce or otherwise exploit a translation needs the authorization of both the owner of copyright in the original and of the owner of copyright in the translation. If only one of these necessary authorizations is obtained, the other copyright owner may act for infringement against that third party.

If a third party reproduces or otherwise exploits the translation with no authorization from either the owner of copyright in the original or the owner of copyright in the translation, both sets of copyright are infringed and each of the copyright owners may bring legal actions against the infringer. However, in certain cases this basic rule may not apply. First, the translator may have been authorized to make the translation together with an agreement to transfer the resulting copyright in the translation to the owner of copyright in the original. In this case, only the owner of copyright in the original may act against unauthorized reproductions or exploitation of the translation, since such owner is the assignee of the exploitation rights in the translation. The translator retains the relevant moral rights and may act against conduct which infringes such rights. Second, the translator may have been authorized to make the translation and to engage in certain acts of exploitation of such translation – for instance, reproducing and selling it in a certain country – while assigning copyright in the translation to the owner of copyright in the original. Again, only the owner of copyright in the original may act against unauthorized reproductions or exploitation of the translation, and the translator retains the relevant moral rights. Finally, the owner of copyright in the original may have not only authorized the translation but also assigned copyright in the underlying work – generally or with regard to translated versions of such work – to the translator. In this case, only the translator may bring legal actions against the infringer, although the author of the original work retains the relevant moral rights in that work and may act against violations of such rights.

Copyright in a translation includes the right of translation of such translation; this is a consequence of the general rules on the right of translation, described in 3.3 above. Since the owner of copyright in the original retains his or her right of translation – unless it has been transferred to the translator – an indirect translation requires the authorization of both the owner of copyright in the original and of the owner of copyright in the translation used for the indirect translation. However, indirect translations create difficult evidence problems, if there is a conflict as to whether the translation was made directly from the original or through an intermediate translation.

If copyright in the original falls in the public domain, particularly because the duration of copyright protection has expired, copyright in the translation remains in place. In other words, the duration and other aspects of copyright protection of the translation are independent from the duration and existence of copyright in the original. Hence, it is possible to obtain copyright protection in works which were already in the public domain at the time the translation was made. The fact that the original has fallen in the public domain means that third parties may freely translate such original, since the extinction of copyright in the original implies that the right of translation of such original has also expired. The fact that a translator had to pay for an authorization under the now expired right of translation gives such translator no right to recoup the payments made or to prevent new translations by persons who don't have to make any payments.

3.6 Term of protection

The general rules on the term of protection of copyright, described in 2.15 above, are applicable to translations. Theoretically, individual countries may enact special rules applicable to the term of copyright protection of translation, provided they comply with the minimum protection terms required by the Berne Convention. In practice, such special rules are rare, and the same duration applies to copyright in translation and to copyright in general. However, as will be analysed in 3.7, individual countries sometimes provide specific rules on limitations on and exceptions from copyright in translation, that may result in shorter effective terms of protection for translations.

The duration of copyright protection of translations is independent from the duration of copyright protection of the translated work. Suppose that XX has written a novel, later translated by YY. A hypothetical country A grants copyright protection for a term of fifty years after the author's death. XX dies on December 31, 2008 and YY on December 31, 2009. Copyright in the novel would extend until December 31, 2058 and on the translation until December 31, 2059. If YY dies before XX, copyright in the translation expires before copyright in the original work, although the translation is a derivative work created after the original.

If a translation enters the public domain, particularly due to expiration of the term of protection, and the translated work is still protected by copyright, unauthorized third parties would still be prevented from reproducing or otherwise exploiting the translation, since the original work is still protected and reproduction or exploitation of the translation constitutes an infringement of copyright in the original.[9] But there would be no civil or criminal actions for violation of copyright in the translation, as that copyright has ceased to exist; only the owner of copyright in the original would be entitled to file legal actions for infringement of that copyright.

3.7 Limitations on and exceptions from copyright in translation

The legal effects of copyright are subject to different limitations and exceptions, which have been described in 2.16 above. Many of these limitations and

---

[9] Under U.S. law, see Grove Press, Inc. v. Greenleaf Publishing Co., 247 F.Supp. 518 (E.D.N.Y. 1965).

exceptions apply to all types of copyrightable intellectual works, and therefore they also bear on copyright in translations. For example, the fair use doctrine, applicable under U.S. law, extends to copyright in translations.

In addition, specific limitations and exceptions have been developed, both in international law and in domestic laws, with regard to translations. The following examples may be mentioned:

- Under Article 2(4) of the Berne Convention, official translations of texts with a legislative, administrative or legal content may be excluded by the member countries from copyright protection.
- Article 2(8) of the Berne Convention allows member countries to exclude copyright protection of news of the day and miscellaneous facts used as press information. Member countries may extend this exception to translations, since generally it can only become effective by means of that extension.
- Article 2*bis*(1) of the Berne Convention allows the exclusion of copyright protection by member countries of political speeches and speeches delivered in the course of legal proceedings. This exception does not automatically extend to translations of such speeches but some countries may proceed to such extension. It should be noted that the effectiveness of the exception does not require its extension to translations, since speeches which have already been translated may be freely translated independently in different versions.
- Lectures, addresses and texts delivered in public may be subject to limitations on copyright protection, if the use made of such materials is restricted to excerpts used for information purposes. This exception to the rules on copyright protection is authorized by Article 2*bis*(2) of the Berne Convention, and member countries may extend it to translated versions of the relevant materials.
- Article 10(1) of the Berne Convention allows member countries to introduce exception to copyright protection with regard to quotations, within the limits of fair use. Member countries frequently make use of these authorizations, extending it both to original texts and to translations. Some countries provide quantitative limits for this exception while others apply the broader and more flexible limits inherent in the fair use doctrine.
- Another set of exceptions applies to the use of texts as illustrations for teaching purposes; these texts may be in their original language or in translation. Article 10(2) of the Berne Convention allows member countries to include these exceptions in their laws, within the limits of fair practice.
- As has been described in 2.19 above, the Berne Convention provides special rules in benefit of developing countries, allowing such countries

to grant licences for the reproduction and circulation of certain types of work, particularly translations. The purpose of these exceptions was to facilitate the access by nationals of developing countries to works with educational purpose, which is commonly the case with translations of texts and other materials used for education. However, these rules are so convoluted and procedurally complex that they have had very little impact on the actual effects of copyright in developing countries.

– Some countries provide broad limitations bearing on copyright of works which have become unavailable in the market. Some of these limitations only apply when the author of the work has died, and thus bear on the author's heirs or assignees. The purpose of these limitations is often to surmount the difficulties publishers may have in locating the heirs or present owners of copyright in works by dead authors and therefore the limitations do not deprive such heirs and owners from their copyright but rather allow the publication of the works of a deceased author, without authorization of the copyright owners, but allowing such owners to claim royalties or a proper remuneration once they become aware of the unauthorized publication. These exceptions apply both to original works and to translations. Certain countries expressly provide an authorization to translate works by dead authors, after a certain period has passed from the death of the author, allowing the owners of copyright in the original a right to a proper remuneration.[10]

3.8 Infringement of copyright in translations. Applicable remedies

The general rules on infringement and remedies applicable to copyright in general – described in 2.17 above – extend to copyright in translations. The owner of copyright in a translation may file civil claims against infringers of his or her copyright without requesting the participation of the owner of copyright in the original or requiring this owner's assent. The same principle applies to criminal remedies, in the countries in which they are possible and depend on the filing of claims by the copyright owner. The owner of copyright in the original has a separate and independent set of claims and remedies. The damages suffered by both copyright owners are subject to separate claims, and each owner has the right to be indemnified for the damages he or she has suffered, independently from the indemnification rights of the other copyright owner.

---

[10] See, for example, Article 6 of the Argentine Copyright Law.

3.9 Contracts related to copyright in translations

The fact that translations constitute derivative works for copyright purposes has several effects on the contractual framework in which translations normally take place. For a translation not to violate the right of translation in the translated work (see 3.3 above) it is necessary for the translation to be authorized by the owner of copyright in the translated work, unless this work is in the public domain. This authorization normally takes place by means of contracts.

A contract authorizing a translation may permit translations into any language or be limited to a specific language. If the authorization mentions a specific language, this will normally imply that translations into other languages are not authorized.

The authorization to translate a work may be subject to other types of restriction. The owner of copyright in the underlying work may limit his or her authorization to the actual translation of the work, without permitting the publication of such translation. However, if the licensee has to pay for the authorization it will normally be implied that the licensee has the right of economic exploitation – specially, reproduction – of the translation, since otherwise that translation would have no economic value. It is also possible for the authorization of the publication or marketing of the translation to be limited, either geographically, or to certain markets – such as books in electronic format – or in other ways – for instance, authorizing the publication of a limited number of copies of the translation.

Certain aspects of the contractual authorization of translations are dealt with in different ways by the various legal systems found in comparative law.

With regard to gratuitous authorizations to publish translations, it has been understood, under English law, that such authorizations may be revoked by giving notice to the licensee (see Bently 1993:526–527). In civil law systems, gratuitous authorizations are generally considered to be contractual transactions, and such authorization may not be unilaterally revoked without a proper cause.

If an authorization regarding a translation has expired, the licensee loses the right to reproduce or otherwise exploit the translation. However, some legal systems allow the licensee to market copies of the translation that were validly manufactured while the authorization was in place.

In the case of authorizations granted in exchange for valuable consideration, generally the licensor does not have the right to revoke or terminate the authorization except as provided in the relevant agreement. If the licensor revokes the authorization in spite of this limitation, the revocation will generally be considered as having no effect, and the licensee may continue with the exploitation of the translation authorized by the original agreement as if the illegal revocation had not taken place. Nevertheless, the different national legal systems allow the licensor to terminate the agreement and the authorization granted thereby if the licensee materially breaches the terms of the agreement, particularly in cases of lack of payment of the royalties or other consideration agreed by the parties.

Special difficulties arise in the case of licences or other authorizations granted by the owner of copyright in the translation. For example, that owner may authorize a film producer to use the translation in a movie. A licence by the owner of copyright in the translation is not sufficient to permit the film producer to thus use that translation; it is also necessary to obtain the authorization of the owner of copyright in the translated work. The owner of copyright in the translation is not liable for these limits bearing on the effects of his or her authorization, unless the translated character of the version delivered to the producer was not made clear or the rights of the owner of copyright in the translation were otherwise misrepresented.

The owner of copyright in the translated work may grant a licence to the translator not only to translate the original work but also to reproduce or otherwise exploit the translation. This right does not automatically imply that the licensee has the right to grant sublicences to third parties, authorizing them to reproduce or exploit the translation. For these sublicences to be possible, they must be expressly authorized by the licensor of the translated work or considered to be implied under the circumstances of the legal relationship between such licensor and the translator, pursuant to the applicable law. Generally, sublicences of the type described in this paragraph imply that once the original licence expires, the sublicences granted thereunder also expire. Hence a sublicensee having the translator's authorization to reproduce or exploit the relevant translation may find that such reproduction or exploitation is no longer possible due to the fact that such sublicensee no longer has an authorization attributable to the owner of copyright in the translated work.

The general aspects of contracts related to translations, such as their formation, effects and enforcement, will be discussed in Chapter 6.

CASE STUDIES

A. X, a translator, has been authorized to translate a work whose copyright owner is Y. Z, a publisher, obtains a licence from X to publish X's translation, but it does not obtain an authorization from Y. Upon the publication by Z of the translation, Y brings an action against Z for violation of Y's copyright in the translated work.

Comments: Z's publication implies reproducing not only X's translation but also the translated work. Therefore, Z requires Y's authorization to publish the translation. Y's authorization to translate does not imply an authorization to grant licences to third parties to reproduce or otherwise exploit the translation or the translated work. Generally, X will not be liable for Z's violation of Y's copyright in the translated work, unless X has misrepresented to Z his or her rights regarding Y's copyright. Z knew or should have known that the authorization of the owner of copyright in the translated work was necessary for the publication of a translation of that work.

B. García, the author of a famous novel in Spanish, authorizes Jones to translate the novel into English and to publish the resulting translation. Several years afterwards, García gives a similar authorization to Smith. Smith makes his own independent translation and publishes it. Jones brings an action against García and Smith for violation of Jones's copyright and contractual rights.

Comments: García's authorization to Jones is not exclusive unless the contractual arrangements provide such exclusivity or the exclusive character of the authorization may be implied from other elements, such as García's representations to Jones. Smith has a separate and valid right to translate and publish an independent translation of García's novel. Smith does not infringe Jones's copyright provided Smith's translation is the result of Smith's independent work.

C. Van Tuyne translates texts and documents for lawyers and businesses. She uses software she has acquired from Trudeau, which she has adapted for her work. She hires Luder to work on the translations generated by that software so as to produce final versions and correct any mistakes that may have resulted in the computer-generated translations. Who owns the copyright in these translations?

Comments: The fact that Van Tuyne has prepared the software used for the computer-generated translation and that she controls the operation of such software will generally be deemed sufficient to consider her as author of the translations. However, Luder should be considered as joint author, since significant creative elements of the final version of the translations are the result of Luder's activity. Luder's copyright as joint author will belong to Van Tuyne, who has hired Luder to participate in the translation work, but Luder will retain the moral rights in the resulting translations, unless such moral rights have been assigned in the countries in which such assignments are possible.

4. Protection of Translations by Confidentiality

4.1 The functions of confidentiality in the area of translation

Translations embody and communicate information. It is a function of translations to convey certain "meanings", expressed in one language, by means of the target language. In addition, a translation implies certain idiomatic information: the "equivalence" between a text in the original language and a text in the target language.

Several parties may be interested in these different types of information. The "meaning" subject to translation may have commercial, technical or personal value. It may refer to trade secrets or to information of a personal character, or for other reasons – such as national defence or security – it may be classified or otherwise restricted as to its disclosure or circulation. Translation makes this information available to an enlarged set of individuals, beginning with the translator and potentially including the persons who may have access to the resulting translation.

From a different perspective, translation requires an investment of money and effort. If a person could use another's translation for such person's needs, that user would be profiting from the translator's efforts, without payment. This type of parasitic conduct distorts the market incentives for translation work. Special legal answers to this problem are required, since the mere use of a translation may be beyond the reach of the copyright protection of that translation.

The legal systems have developed a complex set of rules applicable to the protection of confidential information. These rules apply in addition to those that create intellectual property rights or other types of legal protection – such as contractual rights – applicable to translations.

Confidential information is part of translation work both as an input and as an output. A translator receives a text which embodies certain information and that information may be classified or confidential for various legal reasons. The translator then generates a text in a different language which embodies a similar information and which, in addition, has a certain linguistic relationship with the original text, such relationship having a significant cost and market value. The rules on confidentiality apply both at the input and the output level.

This chapter will describe the main aspects of the legal systems applicable to the protection of confidentiality, in the context of the use and effects of such protection in connection with translations.

4.2 Terminology

Even in the context of a single language – English in our case – the legal terminology applied in relation with the legal protection of confidential information has been ambiguous and variable. One reason for these characteristics is the lack of a coherent set of statutory or judicial rules applicable in this area. In other intellectual property fields, the law has been developed on the basis of coherent statutory frameworks, and this has tended to unify and maintain the terminology used in such fields. But the law on confidentiality is the result of case law based on various types of statutes or on common law, depending on the type of legal system involved. These statutes and judicial precedents use a very heterogeneous terminology, even within each national legal system.

The rules on confidentiality apply to information or knowledge. Originally, both in civil law countries and in legal systems based on the Anglo-American tradition, the focus was on knowledge; the expression *know-how* was used in this context, and in fact it passed, untranslated, into other languages, such as French and Spanish. In recent decades, this usage has changed, and emphasis is now on the idea of information and the different categories thereof. Thus, Article 39 of the TRIPs Agreement, one of the main international provisions in this area, refers to "undisclosed information".

The legal status of information varies considerably depending on the degree to which it has been maintained secret or has been disclosed. A first distinction is between disclosed information and confidential or undisclosed information. Confidential or undisclosed information is such if it is subject to reasonable steps – which may be legal or physical – to keep it secret. Confidentiality is basically a subjective element, whose existence depends on the steps taken by the person having control over the relevant information. Disclosed information does not meet these conditions.

A second distinction is between secret and non-secret information. Secret information consists of confidential information which is not generally known among or readily accessible to persons within the circles that normally deal with the kind of information in question. Secrecy is thus an objective element, resulting from the fact that certain information is not within the reach of persons who work in the field in which such information is used. The fact that certain information is not only confidential but also, objectively, a secret, has significant legal consequences. Secrets enjoy a stronger degree of protection. The violation of certain secrets may result in criminal penalties. Also, information which is not objectively a secret is, by definition, part of the knowledge and technical capabilities of persons working in the field in which such information is used, and contractual or other restrictions on the use of that information may be considered as an unacceptable interference with a person's exercise of his or her labour capacity and professional knowledge.

A third distinction is between trade secrets and other confidential information. Traditionally, the law on confidential information was based on the protection of trade secrets. These include secret information used for commercial or other business purposes. However, in the last decades the structure of this legal area has shifted towards a broader enforcement of the protection of confidential information. Legal protection has been extended not only to secrets but also to confidential information in general. The concept of trade secrets has been enlarged so as to include any kind of business secret or of secrets having commercial or economic value. New legal mechanisms have been developed to protect confidential information of a personal nature, regardless of its market value, such as personal data.

Unfortunately, the result of these developments is that the legal terminology in this area is especially variable and confusing, both in English and in other languages. Although the conceptual and terminological development described in this section has been experienced throughout the world, it has separate manifestations in the different legal systems and terminologies. Some legal systems cling to the somewhat old-fashioned terminology based on the concept of trade secret, because such terminology is used in statutory provisions, and it is these provisions which make up the basis of the enforceable law.

4.3   Confidentiality protection throughout the world

The law on confidential information is part of intellectual property law, but is based on legal techniques which are quite different from those generally applied in the intellectual property area.[1]

One major difference is that most countries lack a comprehensive statutory formulation of the law on confidential information. In the case of other intellectual property rights, most developed legal systems have specific statutory systems which set down the basic framework of each intellectual property right; this is generally the case with patents, trademarks and copyright. Regarding these rights, a basic statutory framework is enforced and further developed by means of a complex set of case law, regulations and other elements, whose composition varies from country to country. But in the field of confidential information, normally there is no basic statute providing the general structure of such information's protection.

Another significant difference relates to the type of rights held by persons having control over confidential information. These persons have the right to prevent other persons from having unauthorized access to such confidential information or from using such information beyond the limits for which use was authorized by the person lawfully controlling the information. But this person does not have the right to prevent the independent creation of the same

---

[1] With regard to the protection of confidential information in the different legal systems of the world, see MacLaren (1997).

information, nor the right to prevent the circulation of the information once it has been made available to the public. In particular, if certain information becomes available to third parties because it is embodied in certain marketed goods and these third parties have been able to reproduce the information through reverse engineering, it is not possible for the original holder of the information to prevent the further use and circulation of that information. The situation is different, especially in the case of patents, where the patent holder can prevent the use or exploitation of the invention during the whole term of the patent, regardless of how potential users have become acquainted with the invention.

These characteristics and limitations of confidentiality protection have created several conceptual and terminological difficulties. It has been debated whether persons having control over confidential information have the "property" of such information. The international rules applicable in this area tend to avoid the use of words such as "property" or "owner" of information, in part due to the lack of consensus about whether such words are properly applicable in this field. From an economic point of view, confidential information has value and works as an asset of the persons lawfully holding such information. It may be the subject matter of contractual transactions, such as assignments and licences, and be exchanged for a valuable consideration. But there is no exclusive right to confidential information, in the sense that it may be reproduced and used by new legitimate holders, particularly by means of independent development. From this perspective the rights of the lawful holder of confidential information are different from those of the holders of intellectual "property" rights such as patents. Summarizing this debate, the rights on confidential information may be characterized or not as property rights depending on the legal system involved and the terminology it adopts, and on which of the different meanings of property is applied. Generally, the rights of the lawful holders of confidential information do not have the degree of exclusiveness characteristic of real property and of traditional intellectual property rights, such as patents, but they are property in the sense of being a subject matter protected from unauthorized access by third parties and having an economic value.

As in other areas of intellectual property, several agreements to which most of the countries of the world are parties establish basic standards of legal protection of confidential information. These standards are far less detailed and demanding than those applicable to patents and other intellectual property rights. One reason for this approach is that it is practically difficult for one country and its nationals to profit from another country's confidential information; the infringers would face the obstacles and sanctions provided by the legal system applicable in his country where the confidential information is located. Also, if a given country provides weak protection to confidential information, the holders of such information will be reluctant to bring it within such country's jurisdiction. From both perspectives, the consequences of weak legal protection of confidential information bear immediately on the country having such weakness, making it less necessary to create additional incentives for adequate protection by way of international standards.

The international standards of legal protection of confidential information focus on the rules on unfair competition applicable in connection with such information. But as will be shown in this chapter, the legal protection of confidential information by the different national legal systems is much broader than that resulting from unfair competition law.

Article 39(1) of the TRIPs Agreement provides that, "in the course of ensuring effective protection against unfair competition" as provided by the Paris Convention – on industrial property – "Members shall protect undisclosed information in accordance with paragraph 2" of the same Article 39. This paragraph 2 in turn provides:

> Natural and legal persons shall have the possibility of preventing information lawfully within their control from being disclosed to, acquired by, or used by others without their consent in a manner contrary to honest commercial practices so long as such information (a) is secret in the sense that it is not, as a body or in the precise configuration and assembly of its components, generally known among or readily accessible to persons within the circles that normally deal with the kind of information in question; (b) has commercial value because it is secret; and (c) has been subject to reasonable steps under the circumstances, by the person lawfully in control of the information, to keep it secret.

In addition, the official footnote to this paragraph indicates that

> For the purpose of this provision, "a manner contrary to honest commercial practices" shall mean at least practices such as breach of contract, breach of confidence and inducement to breach, and includes the acquisition of undisclosed information by third parties who knew, or were grossly negligent in failing to know, that such practices were involved in the acquisition.

Pursuant to these and other international provisions – such as Article 10*bis* of the Paris Convention – provisions have been enacted in the principal legal systems of the world, protecting confidential information from practices characterized as unfair competition. These statutory provisions are frequently highly vague and abstract, and their practical contents result from their judicial interpretation and implementation. In addition, these legal systems have enacted rules beyond their unfair competition regime, with important effects on the protection of confidential information. The overall system of protection of such information results from the interaction between the unfair competition regime and other legal regimes bearing on such information. These different legal components will be examined in the following paragraphs.

4.4 The protection of confidential information by unfair competition law

Unfair competition law is a set of rules which seeks to limit and prevent competition by unfair means, such as providing false information or misappropriating a competitor's resources. Generally, competition is fair if it takes place through the supply of better goods and services at convenient prices, and it may be unfair if competitive advantages are derived otherwise.

Some legal systems, such as those of continental European countries like Spain, Germany and Switzerland, base their unfair competition law on highly comprehensive statutes. Other countries of the civil law tradition, like France or Argentina, do not have comprehensive unfair competition law statutes, and base their unfair competition regimes on the general rules on torts and on different legal provisions applicable to specific unfair competition issues, such as those related to advertisement. In countries of the Anglo-American legal tradition, a combination of statutory rules and judge-made law has been the source of development of the relevant unfair competition rules.

Unfair competition law includes both criminal and civil provisions. Criminal provisions may apply to conduct defined in very broad terms, allowing the courts to specify what is meant by unfair competition under each particular set of circumstances. They may also include penalties specifically applicable to violations related to confidential information which constitute unfair competition. For example, Section 4(9)(c) of the German Unfair Competition Law prohibits certain acts of competition that take place by means of information which has been appropriated from a competitor by dishonest means. These different criminal law provisions included in unfair competition statutes should be distinguished from those directly addressed to information matters, independently from competition considerations, to be described in paragraph 4.5 below. The enforcement of criminal law provisions included in unfair competition statutes tends to be weak, and in some countries wholly inexistent.

Unfair competition law also includes civil remedies. These apply in all cases of unfair competition, even those resulting from very broad definitions not directly concerned with information issues. For example, if a translator, as part of his or her work, obtains certain confidential information which is then misappropriated by a competitor of the person who commissioned the translation, the translator may be civilly liable if that competitor had access to the information due to the translator's negligence or intent. Civil remedies include damages and injunctions, among others.

The unfair competition law protection of confidential information does not apply to all types of conduct that constitute misappropriation of confidential information. For example, such misappropriation may not result in a violation of certain unfair competition laws if the parties involved in such misappropriation – as victims and perpetrators – are not actual competitors. Also, when confidential information is misappropriated as the result of industrial espionage and it is subsequently disclosed to innocent third parties, the owner of such information who is thus damaged may lack action under certain unfair competition laws, which do not extend their rules to industrial espionage.

Very different types of conduct related to confidential information have been considered to fall within the prohibitions derived from unfair competition law. The reasoning behind this extension of unfair competition law to information issues is the following. The person who has access to information by illegal means obtains a competitive advantage derived from the misappropriated information. Hence, both the person using the information and the person illegally providing such information participate in conduct which constitutes unfair competition. Article 39 of the TRIPs Agreement, described in paragraph 4.3 above, follows this approach, describing different types of conduct, related to confidential information, which may constitute unfair competition.

The following are some of the main types of conduct, related to confidential information, that have been considered to fall within the prohibitions derived from unfair competition law.

- <u>Conduct derived from employment relationships</u>. One of the central aspects of confidential information law is that information must be disclosed to employees for it to be put to a productive use, giving them the *de facto* possibility of using or subsequently disclosing that information. To prevent the value of information being eroded by that *de facto* possibility, and to make the exploitation of technology and other information by means of employees practically possible, all developed legal systems have rules on confidential information limiting the disclosure or use of information acquired in the course of employment for purposes other than that employment. Several types of illegal conduct based on employment relationship may be distinguished in connection with the use or disclosure of confidential information, such as disclosure of trade secrets to competitors of the employer, whether during or after the employment relationship, and exploitation by an employee of trade secrets acquired during the course of his or her employment, whether during or after the employment relationship. Generally, the extent of protection granted to information in these circumstances varies greatly depending on whether the information is simply confidential or constitutes a trade secret, a distinction analysed in 4.2 above. If the information is a trade secret, it is generally possible for the employer to prevent the use and disclosure of such information, by the employee, even after the employment relationship has terminated. But once the information is no longer objectively a trade secret, the former employee is allowed to use it, since that information is considered to be part of the normal technological background of a person active in the relevant productive sectors. For example, if a translator works for an industrial company, and has access, as part of his or her work, to such company's trade secrets, generally such translator will be under the obligation to maintain the secrecy of that information and to not use it for his or her own benefit, even after the employment with the company has finished; but these obligations disappear with regard to information which has become freely available in the relevant market, sometimes identified as information in the public domain.

- Illegal appropriation of documents containing confidential information. The typical situation, in this line of cases, occurs when a person takes possession illegally of a document containing confidential information, and then uses that information for business purposes or discloses that information to another person who then uses it for such person's business purposes. This last person becomes liable if it knew or should have known – acting with adequate diligence – that the information had an illegitimate origin. For example, an employee of a manufacturing company takes hold of certain documents containing valuable secret information. The documents are then delivered to a translator who passes on the valuable information to a third party. If, in the context of these relationships, the translator knew or should have known that the documents had been misappropriated, the translator may be held liable as a wilful or negligent participant in an illegal conduct. The fact that the translator delivered the information to a third party may create a presumption that the translator knew about the value and confidential origin of the information.

- Appropriation of confidential information by means of fraud or duress. A person may have access to confidential information by means of threats or deceits, in the context of negotiations or other relationships between the lawful owner of the information and the person guilty of fraud. If that person then uses that information or allows another person to use it, this may constitute unfair competition. For example, several cases in Germany have dealt with the fraudulent misappropriation of know-how as cases of unfair competition, including one in which a machine was examined under the pretence of being interested in its purchase,[2] and another in which a party misled the employees of the

---

[2] Decision of the *Oberlandesgerichts* of Saxony, Oct. 6, 1925, *Markenschutz und Wettbewerb*, 26:57.

enterprise holding the know-how into believing he was a lawyer for that enterprise.[3]
- Appropriation of confidential information in the context of negotiations. It is common for parties negotiating the terms of contractual transactions to disclose to the other party confidential information, so as to allow such other party the possibility of evaluating the convenience or terms of the possible transaction. It is possible and common to enter into so-called precontractual confidentiality agreements, in which the parties agree not to disclose or use the information they receive in the context of these negotiations. Even in the absence of these confidentiality agreements, the party receiving the information is under the obligation to keep it confidential and not to use it for such party's benefit, on the basis of the general rule that confidential information disclosed with a specific purpose may not be used by the recipient beyond the limits of such purpose; the confidentiality agreements, in this context, help to create a more clear and explicit framework for the use of the information exchanged during the precontractual negotiations, and to make the consequences of the violation of the resulting confidentiality obligations more precise and sometimes more severe. If the recipient of the confidential information breaches the limits applicable to the use and disclosure of that information, such conduct may constitute unfair competition, and the same result may extend to third parties who have access to that information knowing that it was misappropriated in the course of negotiations or ignoring that characteristic due to their negligence. This type of liability may result when a text to be translated, embodying confidential information, is disclosed to a translator in the course of negotiations about the price and other terms of possible future translation work.
- Appropriation of confidential information as a consequence of contractual relationships. Information may be transferred as part of contractual relationships between the transferor and the transferee, with a purpose other than the unrestricted disclosure of such information in favour of the transferee. For example, information may be disclosed to a subcontractor to make possible the performance of its obligations towards the main contractor; or a translator may have access to a text including business secrets for purposes of performing the relevant translation work. In these cases, it is generally understood that, regardless of the existence or not of contractual clauses expressly limiting the transferee's rights as to the disclosed information, such

---

[3] Decision of the *Reichsgericht*, Jan. 21, 1913, *Markenschutz und Wettbewerb*, 12:509.

transferee is under an obligation to not use the information beyond the scope of the purpose for which it was disclosed, and to not disclose it to third parties unless such disclosure is necessary for purposes of performing the obligations resulting from the relevant agreement. Use or disclosure beyond these limits may constitute unfair competition and the same result may extend to a third party who – acting in bad faith – further uses or transfers the information it has received from a party who is acting in breach of the limits applicable to the information disclosed in the context of previous contractual relationships.

- Appropriation of information in the context of corporate or partnership relationships. The use or exploitation of information by a partnership or a corporation may require its disclosure to partners or corporate officers who are not immediately bound by the restrictions bearing on employees of such firms. Partnerships and corporations are separate legal entities with their own rights over their technology and other valuable information. Hence, when their partners or officers have access to information owned by their firms, they must use that information within the limits of the purposes for which such access is given, and they must preserve the confidentiality of that information. Also, if technology or other information is acquired by a third party in the course of the winding-up of an enterprise, the partners or corporate officers who had access to that technology or information during the existence of that enterprise may be enjoined from subsequently using it. The breach of these different limits may result in conduct constituting unfair competition. For example, a translator has access to a company's secret know-how for purposes of translation. The company is afterwards liquidated, and its different assets – including the secret know-how – sold as part of the liquidation. After such sales, one of the company's directors obtains from the translator information about the secret know-how, on the grounds that such director had helped develop the know-how during the company's operation. The director may be guilty of unfair competition – and the translator of being a participant in such act – since he or she never had a property right over the secret know-how, which belonged to the company and not to its directors.
- Appropriation of information in other confidential contexts. Generally, when information is disclosed with a specific purpose, the transferee must refrain from using or disclosing such information beyond what is necessary for that purpose. Therefore, there is a wide variety of circumstances in which a confidentiality obligation as to information may be broken, leading to a situation of unfair competition resulting from the exploitation or use of the misappropriated information. For example, if know-how is revealed to a potential creditor for purposes

of ascertaining the solvency of a possible future debtor, such creditor may not use that know-how for other purposes.[4]

4.5 The criminal law protection of confidential information

In many countries, the illegal appropriation or communication of confidential information is treated as a punishable offence. This treatment may apply both to conduct by employees and to conduct by other persons who infringe the rights of the person who lawfully controls the information.

In the context of U.S. law, MacLaren (1997:A1–35) indicates that criminal statutes which make it a crime to steal trade secrets have been enacted in many states, adding

> These state laws recognize that trade secrets are property, the theft of which can be covered by criminal statutes. The general thrust of these trade secrets laws is the intentional misappropriation of trade secrets. If intent is established, the resulting harm done to the trade secret owner is immaterial. This approach is different from that taken in civil trade secret cases, where the measure of damages is essentially the harm done to the trade secret owner.

There are several variations of these criminal rules. In many countries, the criminal law protection of information only applies to technology that is a trade or industrial secret; it will not apply to technology that is kept confidential but which does not meet the objective criteria necessary to qualify as a trade secret, described in 4.2 above, nor to information that has no industrial or business application. However, conduct relative to information which does not constitute a trade secret may still be illegal and result in civil liabilities, such as those described in 4.4.

Another variation is based on the distinction between use and disclosure. Some criminal law provisions impose sanctions on the disclosure of information by persons who had the obligation to preserve such information's confidentiality, but not on the appropriation or use of that information by the persons who have access to it.

A third variation has to do with the identity of the person who violates the rules on confidential information. Some laws restrict the criminal nature of infringements to those carried out by persons who have special legal relationships with the person who lawfully controls the information, such as employees or professionals. This sometimes creates odd results. A translator who is given access to certain information, for translation purposes, may be

---

[4] This was the position held in the U.S. case of Barnes v. Cahill, 133 P.2d 433 (2d. Dist. 1943).

subject to criminal penalties if he or she then discloses that information to unauthorized third parties, but a person guilty of industrial espionage would not be subject to criminal penalties since such person had no employment or professional relationship with the information's owner. This has made it necessary to include additional rules addressed to the problems created by industrial espionage. These rules, frequently imposing criminal penalties, address the problem of industrial espionage, that is access to trade secrets and other confidential information by means of theft or misappropriation, by persons who destroy or circumvent the protection which preserves the confidentiality of that information.

Finally, criminal law rules applicable to the protection of confidential information may focus on the technological content of information or on other aspects of the latter. The rules which traditionally have penalized the violation of trade secrets have included requirements as to the economic use to which such secrets are put; only secrets which are applied in business or in other economic activities are subject to protection under some of these rules. The contemporary tendency is to do away with this type of distinction, and to grant criminal law protection to all types of secret or confidential information. Sometimes this extension takes place indirectly, due to the fact that the applicable rules do not focus on the type of information involved but rather on the illegal conduct related to that information. This is the case with criminal law provisions that punish employees who solicit or receive payments from third parties to undertake certain illegal conduct connected with their employment or which impose sanctions on third parties guilty of corrupting employees. It is also the case with the criminal law provisions on abuse of confidence, such as those which punish the misappropriation of goods entrusted to employees.

4.6 Contract law protection of confidential information

Confidential information may be protected by contract in several ways. The protection of that information depends on its status as confidential or secret. This status in turn depends on whether the owner of the information has taken adequate precautions to prevent its disclosure or access to that information by third parties. A person who receives information in the course of such person's employment or of business transactions does not necessarily know whether that information is confidential or subject to restrictions as to its use or disclosure. These restrictions may reasonably result from the circumstances in which the information is received. If an employee has access to certain machinery which is surrounded by major security precautions, that employee should know, in the context of his or her technical qualifications, that the information embodied in that machinery constitutes valuable technical knowledge that should be kept secret. Parties linked by contractual relationships may clearly establish in their contracts the confidential or secret nature of the information to be exchanged in the context of such contractual relationships. In particular, a translator receiving certain information for translation purposes may be informed about the confidential or secret status of that information.

Contracts may also establish the obligation parties to such contracts shall have with respect to the confidentiality of the information to be exchanged in the context of such contracts. A party receiving or having access to confidential information – in particular, a translator – is subject to legal confidentiality obligations even in the absence of contractual provisions creating such obligations. This is the case, especially, with the obligations resulting from the unfair competition and criminal law provisions described in 4.4 and 4.5 above. But the parties may agree that they shall preserve the confidentiality of the information they receive, and limit the use and disclosure of such information, beyond what the preexisting legal rules already provide. Contractual provisions to that effect are generally valid and enforceable.

Different limitations bear on the legal and practical effectiveness of contractual provisions on confidentiality. From a legal point of view, contractual restrictions on the use of information may be judged to be illegal because they affect the right to use publicly known technology or because they prevent a worker from practising his or her trade; in several countries this illegality is considered to result from the violation of the constitutional right to work of the person subject to the contractual restrictions. If the information involved is a trade secret, restrictions are generally considered valid, since that information is not available, by definition, to the average person working in the trade in which the information is used.

Contractual restrictions on the use of information may also be illegal when they have anticompetitive effects which are not justified by the context in which such restrictions are imposed. For example, if a person is given access to certain information, and is prevented from using such information in the service of firms that compete with the firm which supplied that information, this restriction may be deemed unjustified from a competition law perspective once the information has become publicly known other than by action of the person subject to the restriction.

The practical effectiveness of the contractual protection of confidentiality is limited by the fact that such protection is only effective in relation to parties with which the owner of the information has direct contractual relationships; it has no effect against third parties that act in good faith.

Contractual provisions used to protect confidential information are included in very different types of transaction. Contracts with employees are a typical case. These contracts may include obligations not to disclose the information made available to employees in the course of their employment, obligations not to use that information for purposes other than work with the employer, and obligations not to compete with the employer, particularly when such competition would imply the use of information made available to the employee by that employer.

These contractual provisions are also common in transactions with contractors, subcontractors and service providers. In the context of these transactions, information may be transferred to the contractor, subcontractor or service provider for purposes of the performance of these parties' obligations under the agreement. The transferor will normally intend to restrict the transferee's right to use such information for other purposes. This restriction will normally result from the context of the information transfer, without express provisions to that effect, but the transferor may be interested in strengthening, extending or making more precise the transferee's obligations as to the information such transferee receives, or in creating evidence about the information's status. Translators receiving information in the context of translation work not performed as employees would fall within this category.

Confidentiality provisions may also be part of pre-contractual arrangements. When information must be disclosed in the course of negotiations, these arrangements are used to ascertain the rights of the parties as to such information and to strengthen the obligations that may result from the rules governing the conduct of the parties in relation to such negotiations.

Special problems arise in connection with commercial information given to employees, contractors, franchisees and other parties, such as lists of clients, sales methods, distribution channels or marketing procedures. This type of information may create conflicts because of difficulties in determining the rights of the parties as to such information in the absence of contractual arrangements defining them. Although such information may qualify as a trade secret, it may at the same time be acquired as a consequence of the legitimate activities of the employees or other parties involved. This may create difficulties when the original transferor intends to prevent the use of information it has supplied, after termination of the employees', contractors', franchisees' or other parties' activities, either because it is not possible to ascertain the origin of a given piece of information or due to restrictions on provisions preventing a party from using the information necessary for his or her profession or trade. In this context, contractual clauses may specify the nature and limits of the information supplied and the rules applicable to the information obtained or developed by the original transferee in the context of his or her activities.

4.7 Protection of information under the rules on privacy

Different rules have been developed in comparative law for the protection of privacy. In many countries, statutes and case law have defined areas where an individual's life, feelings and information are protected from intrusion by other persons. This extends to matters as diverse as information about a person's health or sexual life or about such person's religious or political inclinations, photographs or personal correspondence.

In recent years, the scope of this protection has been enlarged and strengthened by statutes, enacted in many countries, on personal data protection. Translators, in the context of their work, are subject to the obligations derived from these privacy rules, particularly with regard to the personal information they come across as part of their work. These obligations are legally imposed by virtue of the nature of the information involved and do not require a contractual agreement in which the translator undertakes to preserve the confidentiality of the private information made available in the context of translation work.

Obligations related to personal data may include the prohibition to disclose such information except to the persons and in the cases provided by the applicable rules, the obligation to take the necessary precautions to prevent unauthorized disclosure of access to the information, and compliance with special rules as to the storage, processing or disclosure of the personal data.

4.8 Liabilities for unjust enrichment in connection with the use of information

A person may have access to valuable information, and profit from its use, with the authorization or consent to such access of the information's original legitimate owner, but beyond the limits originally envisioned by such owner. For example, a translator may have access to information about the planned operations of a company, in the context of translation work commissioned by such company, and use the information to enter into profitable transactions, such as buying certain real estate. If the person having access to the information does not act in bad faith, for instance because he or she was not properly notified about the confidential character of the information involved and had no reason to presume confidentiality, it may be impossible to prevent the use of that information. However, the legitimate owner who suffers a damage or loss due to that use may recover an amount equivalent to the profit obtained by the user, on the legal basis of the latter's unjust enrichment.

Under U.S. law, several types of case have been distinguished in connection with liability for unjust enrichment resulting from the use of information (Dessemontet 1976:349–350). In the first group of cases, unsolicited information is disclosed to a person – for example, a translator, for purposes of preparing a cost estimate of a translation – who thereafter uses that information without having agreed to the transaction offered by the originator of the information. The second group includes cases in which information is disclosed inadvertently and such information is used without bad faith, that is, without knowledge of the mistake that led to its disclosure. Finally, unjust enrichment may result when employees violate the confidentiality obligations as to know-how which the employer maintains undisclosed under secrecy precautions.

In other countries, the applicability of unjust enrichment rules to conduct related to information is more limited and theoretical. However, the principles of unjust enrichment are practically universal, and may be the basis of liability for the unintended use of confidential information.

4.9 Tort liability as to conduct related to information

The protection of confidential information under tort law principles is of special importance due to the loopholes found in other sources of legal protection of that information. In most countries, the main rules applicable to information are addressed to specific aspects of the use or disclosure of that information: its use in business activities (unfair competition law), its disclosure by employees (labour law and criminal law), etc. This approach leaves the owners of information unprotected in relation to several types of conduct, such as – in many countries –industrial or research espionage.

In jurisdictions of the Anglo-American group, the liability in tort for disclosure or use of another's trade secrets has a long tradition. Section 757 of the Restatement of the Law of Torts, adopted by the American Law Institute, states:

> One who discloses or uses another's trade secret, without a privilege to do so, is liable to the other if (a) he discovered the secret by improper means, or (b) his disclosure or use constitutes a breach of confidence reposed in him by the other in disclosing the secret to him, or (c) he learned the secret from a third person with notice of the facts that it was a secret and that the third person discovered it by improper means or that the person's disclosure of it was otherwise a breach of duty to the other, or (d) he learned the secret with notice of the facts that it was a secret and that its disclosure was made to him by mistake.

These rules have been repeatedly applied by U.S. courts.

English law is vaguer about this matter. Noncontractual liability has been found to exist in relation to trade secrets on the basis of implied noncontractual obligations of trust, confidence and good faith. In the absence of a general system of unfair competition law, actions based on breach of confidence have played a major role in the development of the English rules applicable to trade secrets. However, there has been a strong tendency to base the defendant's liability in such cases on the violation of implied contractual obligations.

The position of confidential information under tort law in civil law countries is even more problematic. These countries generally have broad provisions in their civil codes which apply in principle to all types of illegal conduct which cause damage to another person or to his or her property, and which could therefore be considered applicable to the damages caused by an illegal use or disclosure of information. However, in the absence of definite statutory provisions defining illegal conduct in relation to information and of sufficient case law applying to information matters, it is not possible to derive clear conclusions about the precise applicability of tort provisions in this area. The rights held by the rightful owner of information must be derived from other rules – such as those that govern employment relationships – and tort law becomes applicable once such rights are violated. In the last decades, several civil law countries have enacted legislation establishing the basic rights and obligations regarding confidential information; these rules permit more accurate and consistent enforcement of the general tort rules applicable to information matters.

4.10 Labour law protection of information

Both civil law countries and jurisdictions of the Anglo-American legal system have enacted multiple statutory rules in connection with the rights to information developed in or used in the context of employment relationships.

Since much of the valuable information developed in modern societies is generated in the context of employment relationships, it is of the utmost importance in this legal area to determine the respective legal rights of employers and employees. Generally, employers own the information generated by employees hired with the purpose of producing that information. Information generated by employees outside the scope of their employment and with their own means belongs to the employees. In cases falling in between these two categories, legal systems apply special rules to information generated by employees on the basis of the information they had access to in the course of their employment, or which is related to the employees' work or which has been obtained using the means provided by the employer. It is common for these legal systems to attribute ownership of information falling in these intermediate categories to the employer or to grant such employer the option to acquire rights to the information; but if the employee does not retain property of this information, the employer generally has to make payment in addition to the employee's salary, since by definition the employee has not developed this information in the context of the work for which he or she was hired and paid.

Labour law rules also restrict the unauthorized use or disclosure of information, acquired by employees during the course of their employment, during or after the course of that employment. The effects of these restrictions vary depending on the status of the information involved. If the information objectively constitutes a trade secret – according to the conditions described in 4.2 above – the restrictions extend even after the employment relationship has expired, and they apply not only to the disclosure of the trade secret but also to the use of that information by the former employee, individually or in the context of a new employment. If the information does not objectively constitute a trade secret, it is generally possible for the employer to direct the employee to preserve it as confidential, at least while the employment relationship in the context of which the information was disclosed still continues. Once such relationship finishes, the employee is generally free to use or disclose information which does not constitute a trade secret, even if the employer wishes to maintain that information as confidential. Contractual clauses limiting employees' rights regarding this information may be considered invalid, particularly if they are deemed to be excessively broad or durable in the context of the adequate protection of the employer's legitimate interests.

It is common, in the context of employment relationships, for employers to negotiate with their employees changes in the basic legal framework described in this paragraph or contractual rules related to the application of such legal rules. Sometimes, agreements of this type do not intend to modify the parties' original rights, but rather to facilitate their enforcement and effectiveness. For example, contractual clauses may define what information should be considered confidential by the employees and clarify the employees' obligations as to that information, even though the employees' confidentiality obligations would result even in the absence of such contractual arrangements. In some cases, the effects of contractual arrangements on confidentiality are indirect. In particular, if an employee is subject to contractual non-compete obligations, compliance with these obligations may prevent the employee from using previously acquired information with a new employer.

These different contractual employer–employee arrangements are frequently subject to strict limitations derived from labour law rules or principles. In many countries, the employee has a set of minimum statutory rights which may not be reduced contractually. Therefore, employer–employee agreements may strengthen the employee's statutory rights, but not limit them. For example, if an employee is the owner of certain information, according to the rules on ownership of such information previously described in this paragraph, the employer may not limit or deny such rights by means of a contractual arrangement which transfers all such rights to the employer.

4.11 Miscellaneous legal sources of protection of information

It is not possible to make an exhaustive description of the legal rules and principles applicable to the protection of information. These rules vary significantly from one legal system to the other, and are commonly placed in very different and apparently unrelated statutory and regulatory provisions, such as patent laws and rules on administrative procedures. However, certain legal sources of information protection may be especially relevant for translators.

In many countries, the activities of translators are governed by special statutes determining who may legally act as a translator, who and in what conditions may legally certify translations, and other aspects of the organization and practice of the profession. These statutes frequently include rules stating that translators are under the obligation of maintaining as confidential the information they obtain in the course of their professional practice.

Also, procedural rules and statutes may create confidentiality obligations as to the information obtained by professionals who participate in legal procedures. This is the case with court translators and interpreters.

In addition, administrative rules govern the documentation used in governmental procedures, and these rules may include provisions on confidentiality and secrecy, which may extend to translators acting in the context of such procedures.

4.12 The effects of confidentiality obligations on translations

Given the complexity and reach of the confidentiality rules described in this chapter, it is immediately obvious that confidentiality obligations may have very different effects on the activities of translators and on the resulting translations. These effects will vary depending on multiple circumstances, such as the legal status of the information involved – discussed in 4.2 above – the context in which the information is delivered to the translator and the contractual relationships which link the translator to other parties.

A translator receiving information for translation purposes – such as a text or a legal document – is immediately subject to the confidentiality rules imposed by the professional regulations applicable to translators. In some countries, these regulations impose a general confidentiality obligation to translators with regard to the material they have access to in the course of their work. In addition, translators are subject to obligations resulting from the confidential nature of the information they receive. If the information is confidential, the translator will generally have the obligation not to use it or disclose it beyond what is necessary for the purposes for which the information was delivered, namely the translation of the text including the relevant information.

A basic problem, in connection with these obligations, derived from the confidential character of information, is how the translator determines that the information he or she receives is confidential. This confidential character may result expressly from the legal relationships between the information's transferor and transferee. The transferor may inform the transferee – in this case, the translator – that the information is confidential, and this may be enough to create a confidentiality obligation bearing on the translator. In addition, the transferor and the transferee may be part of a contractual transaction in which the transferee – the translator – is under the obligation to keep the information received in the context of that transaction as confidential.

The translator may be subject to confidentiality obligations resulting from the confidential status of information even in the absence of contractual provisions or express indications by the transferor to the effect that the information is confidential. If the translator knew or should have known that the information is confidential, he or she must treat it as such. The translator may know that the information is confidential because of different elements related to that information: warning signs included with the documents through which the information is conveyed, the translator's knowledge about the nature of the operations of the person conveying the information, among other possibilities. Also, there are multiple reasons why the translator, as transferee of information, may be considered to be in the position of having to know, if acting diligently, the confidential status of the information. If the lawful owner of information prevents access to such information by means of costly and generally obstructive measures whose purpose clearly is to prevent such access, persons who come in contact with the information and with the means which protect it from access by unauthorized parties are generally under the obligation to preserve its confidentiality, on the basis that they should have known the confidential character of the information thus protected. For example, if certain documents are kept in safes, access to which is limited to certain key employees, a person – such as a translator – having access to such documents for specific purposes – in this case, translation work – will normally be considered as knowing or having the duty to know that such documents include confidential information.

Once it is determined that certain information received by the translator is confidential, the translator will be subject to different obligations. The translator may not use the information for purposes other than the translation work he or she was hired for, and may not disclose the information to other parties. However, there are several limits on these basic obligations. The translator may not be prevented from using information which is generally available. In other words, if information is no longer a trade secret or is part of the common knowledge in the field in which it is applied, use of that information may not be restricted. In these cases, the person receiving the information could have obtained it from other sources and therefore the person delivering the information to a translator cannot argue that the translator uses the information by virtue of the commissioned translation work.

Similarly, if information is part of the stock of knowledge available to normally trained persons acting in the field in which that information is used – implying that the information is not a trade secret – that information may be used in the course of employment by a third party. The fact that the information is not a trade secret will lead to giving legal priority to the employee's or potential employee's right to practise his or her trade, vis-à-vis the rights of the information owner.

It may happen that information is delivered to a transferee such as a translator, protected by valid limitations on the use of that information, on the basis that the information is a trade secret, but that the trade secret status of the information disappears with the passage of time. In such cases, the limitations are initially valid but lose their legal effectiveness once the information becomes publicly known; the transferee will then need to use the information for the normal practice of his or her trade, and the original owner of the information will lose the legitimate interest such owner may have had in limiting the circulation of information which is now part of the public domain.

With regard to limitations on disclosure, the degree to which they are considered valid varies depending on their origin and on the status of the information involved. If the limitations result from the operation of the law, normally they will only be effective with regard to information which is a trade secret and for as long as that information retains that condition. If the restrictions are imposed by contractual provisions, generally they are valid provided there is a legitimate reason from maintaining their effects. These possible legitimate reasons tend to disappear once the information ceases to be a trade secret, since then it is, by definition, freely available to anyone who hires a person normally trained in the field in which the information is used.

4.13 The protection of translation work by means of confidentiality

Translation generates new information. The meaning of a translated text remains, at least theoretically, unaltered, but the translation embodies information about how that meaning is conveyed in a different language. This information has economic value, since generally it is useful and there is a market for it, and has a cost in terms of the time and effort that must be put into its production. All the elements which explain and justify the legal protection of information are thus present.

Generally, confidentiality is not necessary to preserve the translation's value and the legitimate interests of the translator. The translator's rights are protected by his or her intellectual property in the translation. However, the translator may be interested, for several reasons, in preserving the confidentiality of the translation.

First, the translator may consider that protection from unauthorized reproduction is more effective by means of confidentiality than through copyright. Copyright protection has major practical shortcomings in many countries. Once a text – in this case, a translation – becomes known, it may be practically impossible for the person who wrote that text to prevent its circulation through informal channels. The advent of the Internet has enhanced this danger. Hence, when a translator wishes to prevent the circulation of a translation, he or she may prefer to keep it confidential. This is legally possible and generally does not affect whatever copyright the translator may have on the translation. Nevertheless, if the translator wishes to enforce his or her copyright, the enforcement may terminate the confidential status of the translation, either because the translation has to be registered for purposes of copyright protection – as is still the case in some countries – or because the work has to be disclosed in court or other proceedings.

Second, the translator may be under confidentiality obligations bearing on the text he or she is translating. These confidentiality obligations may be breached not only in the case of the original text being disclosed to unauthorized parties, but also in the case of the translation being thus disclosed or accessed, since the information protected by the hypothetical confidentiality obligations would be conveyed, albeit in a different language, to the unauthorized parties. Therefore, to prevent liabilities, the translator must take reasonable steps to preserve the confidential status of the information, and these steps should result in extending to the translation the confidential status of the original, provided the translator has effectively taken such reasonable steps.

Third, the translator, as author of a work protected by copyright, has different moral rights on the translation, described in 2.14 above. These rights include the right of divulgation, that is, the right to decide whether to publish a work or not. The effectiveness of this right may be protected by preserving the confidential nature of the translation.

Fourth, the translator may have a legitimate interest in preserving his or her translation work as confidential for other reasons related to the effectiveness of copyright protection. Suppose that a translator is working on a lengthy and complex translation, for publication purposes. Until the work is delivered and published – and registered, if that is the case – the translator faces the risk that someone may have access to the work in progress, who may then claim authorship – and the resulting rights – of such work. From a strictly legal point of view, copyright in this work belongs to its real author, but the party who misappropriated the work may claim that he or she is the real author; the conflict is then decided on the basis of the evidence the parties can produce. To prevent this type of risk, the translator may preserve the confidentiality of the translation, and the rules described in this chapter would be applicable.

Whatever the reasons leading to the confidentiality of a translation, such confidentiality is protected by the rules applicable to undisclosed information, described in this chapter. As in other contexts, the extent of such legal protection varies depending on the characteristics of the information involved. Protection will be stronger if the information objectively constitutes a trade secret. In this respect, it is interesting to notice that a translation embodies two different levels of information: the meaning conveyed from one language to the other, and the way that meaning is expressed in the target language. Hence, a translation may constitute a trade secret because it embodies such secret at either of these two levels. For example, the description of an invention may be a secret in its original language and will remain a secret once that description has been translated, provided adequate steps are taken to preserve that secret status in the translated version.

CASE STUDIES

A. Jones, a translator, receives from Continental Everything (CE), a client, the original version of a contract, for translation purposes. Jones has been working for several years with CE and receives, from time to time, different types of document without any indication as to whether they should be kept confidential or contain secret or classified information. In this particular case, the contract to be translated is a joint venture agreement with a major Asian company, for the building and operation of a new plant. Jones leaves a copy of the contract on his desk. A few days after receiving that copy, CE and Jones find that a photocopy of the contract has been made available to a newspaper, which has published an article on the joint venture's plans. As a consequence of this publication the price of CE's stock climbs significantly, and then drops, and a competitor announces that it has decided to build a similar plant. CE blames Jones for the leak.

Comments: CE and Jones face an initial evidence problem: determining how the contract was photocopied and how the photocopy reached the press. If it can be shown that the photocopy was made from the document in Jones's possession – for example, because it had some notes handwritten by Jones – it will be necessary to establish whether Jones is liable for the leak and its consequences. If Jones knew, or should have known in the context of the relevant circumstances, that the document received from CE contained confidential information, Jones will be under the obligation to prevent the unauthorized access by third parties to the document. The fact that Jones did not receive any formal notice from CE as to the confidentiality of the information included in the contract does not eliminate Jones's obligations, since Jones could have determined, on the basis of the document's contents and of his past relationships with CE that the document was to be kept confidential. In addition, it will be necessary to determine whether Jones took the appropriate steps to preserve the confidentiality of the contract. The fact that there was a leak does not immediately make Jones liable, since Jones may have taken adequate steps to protect the document and have such steps circumvented by unusual action by a third party, such as stealing a heavy safe from Jones's premises. However, leaving a copy of the contract on his desk would clearly imply that Jones has not taken adequate precaution to prevent access to the document, and Jones would be liable if it is determined that he knew or should have known that the document included confidential information.

B. Schmitt has been commissioned by the Altrichter Verlag (AV), a German publisher, to translate into German a selection of García Lorca's poems. Schmitt has completed the translation, which has not yet been published by AV. Bauer, another translator, on the occasion of a visit to Schmitt's home, removes a copy of Schmitt's translation. Bauer makes a few changes to Schmitt's translation and sells the modified version of Schmitt's work to Neuschloss Verlag (NV), another German publisher. Before Schmitt or AV take any action, NV publishes Bauer's version. Schmitt wishes to know what rights she has against Bauer and NV.

Comments: Schmitt is the original owner of copyright over her translation of García Lorca's poems even if Bauer's translation is published first. Bauer has infringed Schmitt's right to maintain Schmitt's translation confidential, if it was evident from Schmitt's conduct that it was her intention to preserve such confidentiality until publication. Schmitt's rights based on Bauer's confidentiality breach do not protect Schmitt against NV's publication, if NV acted in good faith, and do not allow Schmitt to prevent the circulation of the copies published by NV on the basis of breach of confidentiality rights. However, Schmitt may exercise her copyright, if she can show that she was the original author of NV's published version, and prevent further sales of such version; she may also obtain damages from Bauer, and eventually from NV if she can show that NV acted with fault or negligence.

C. Cap, a native of Poland, has worked for many years in Tradex S.A., an international marketing company. Cap, a man fluent in several languages, prepared letters, memoranda and other correspondence, as part of his work, in many cases translating drafts prepared in Spanish or English by members of Tradex's staff. Due to the nature of his work, Cap acquired extensive knowledge about Tradex's business, clients and procedures. After leaving his employment with Tradex, Cap is hired by Incommerce Inc., another marketing firm. Tradex finds out about Cap's new employment and wishes to prevent him from using the information on trading business, clients and procedures Cap acquired during his employment with Tradex.

Comments: Generally, under the labour law rules applicable in developed legal systems, Cap, upon leaving his employment with Tradex, would be entitled to put into practice, by himself or in the context of work under a different employer, the knowledge and information he obtained while working for Tradex. In many countries this is considered necessary for the effectiveness of Cap's constitutional right to work. However, several limits could be applicable to Cap's activities in his new job. Cap and Tradex may have agreed, as part of Cap's employment termination, that Cap would not work for a competitor. This type of clause may be valid, though subject to geographical and time limits which vary depending on the applicable national law; many countries impose maximum terms to these non-compete obligations. Also, Cap may be restricted as to using or disclosing information which objectively constitutes a trade secret. For information to have this quality it must be subject to confidentiality obligations – which normally result from the fact that it was acquired in the course of employment – and not be part of the knowledge generally available to persons acting in the trade in which the relevant information is used. In other words, Cap, with regard to the use of previously acquired knowledge, may not be placed in a position worse than that of persons "within the circles that normally deal with the kind of information in question".[5]

---

[5] This is the terminology used, in this context, by Art. 39.2(a) of the TRIPs Agreement.

5. Labour Law Protection of Translations and Translators

5.1 Labour law and its applicability to translations

Much of the translation work performed throughout the world takes place in the context of employer–employee relationships. There are different kinds of business models in which this type of work takes place, for example:

- A publishing firm may hire a translator on a permanent basis for purposes of translating works from or into a given language.
- Some business organizations have, as their principal activity, translating different types of documents, and must hire translators for purposes of carrying out their business.
- Some organizations, such as law firms, which have a constant demand for translation work, may hire one or more translators on a permanent basis, instead of requesting translation work from independent translators.
- A business with significant clerical staff may from time to time request one or more of its employees to translate certain documents.

The fact that a translation takes place in the context of employer–employee relationships has multiple legal effects on the rights in or related to that translation. That fact defines the applicability of a special set of rules determining the ownership of copyright in works created by employees. Also, the fact that information is exchanged in the context of employer–employee relationships bears on the rules applicable to the protection of such information. The rules for the determination of the remuneration of translation work differ depending on whether that work was performed by an employee or not. The possibility of governing by contract the legal relationships between a translator and the person commissioning translation work is very different in the case in which the translator is an employee of such person.

Labour law is far from uniform throughout the world. Although substantial international rules exist in this field, particularly those agreed to in the context of the International Labour Organization, major differences can be found between countries. Generally, countries of the Anglo-American legal system tend to be more permissive of contractual arrangements between employers and employees. Civil law countries tend to enact detailed statutes and regulations governing most aspects of employment relationships, which allow little room for private negotiations, except to the extent that they strengthen the employees' rights; employees are deemed to be in a weak bargaining position which prevents them from negotiating adequately with employers. Also, while the effects of collective bargaining agreements are generally limited, in countries of the Anglo-American legal system, to workers affiliated to the trade unions participating in the negotiation of such agreements, in some civil law countries the effects of collective bargaining agreements may extend to all the workers employed in a given trade, even if they are not members of the trade unions negotiating these agreements.

5.2   The translator as employee

As discussed in 5.1, the fact that a translation is made in the context of employer–employee relationships has a substantial impact on the rules applicable to such translation. Hence, a basic legal issue in the context of translation activities is the determination of whether the translator is an employee of the person who has commissioned the translation.

Different legal systems have developed various rules to determine whether an employment relationship exists. Obviously, if an express employment contract exists it will be generally understood that there is such relationship, with the resulting legal consequences. In the absence of such a contract, different tests are applied.

U.S. law applies the "control test" (Rothstein *et al.* 1994:17 v. 2):

> In many cases, courts emphasize the so-called "control test" to resolve questions regarding the existence or nonexistence of an employment relationship. When the evidence demonstrates that the principal possesses the authority to exercise meaningful control over the individual's performance, courts usually find (an) ... employment relationship. In situations where the principal lacks such authority, excluded independent contractor relationships are normally determined. The critical consideration under the "right-to-control" test concerns the capacity of the principal to regulate the manner and means of job performance. If the principal is merely empowered to specify the final product, but not the way in which it is to be achieved, the control factor would favor an "independent contractor" finding.

U.S. law also applies, in some cases, a somewhat different approach, based on the consideration of several factors, which the courts must weigh and apply in light of the circumstances of each case. This approach has been used, in particular, to determine whether a person is an employee or an independent contractor, for purposes of applying the rules on ownership of intellectual property of works developed by employees (ibid.:227). The Restatement (Second) of Agency – Section 220 – lists the following factors, which have been applied by courts in cases involving copyright of works developed by possible employees:[1]

---

[1] E.g. in M.G.B Homes, Inc. v. Ameron Homes, Inc., 903 F.2d 1486 (11th. Cir. 1990).

- The extent of control which, by the agreement with the hypothetical employee, the master may exercise over the details of the work.
- Whether or not the one employed is engaged in a distinct occupation or business.
- The kind of occupation, with reference to whether, in the locality, the work is usually done under the direction of the employer or by a specialist without supervision.
- The skill required in the occupation.
- Whether the employer or the workman supplies the instrumentalities, tools, and the place of work for the person doing the work.
- The length of time for which the person is employed.
- The method of payment, whether by the hour or by the job (payment by the hour being normally characteristic of employment relationships).
- Whether or not the work is part of the regular business of the employer.
- Whether or not the parties believe they are creating the relation of master and servant.
- Whether the principal is or is not in business.

Civil law countries usually apply a "dependency" test; an employer–employee relationship exists if the hypothetical employee has a "dependency relationship" with the principal. This dependency relationship has three basic elements. First, the employee must work under the orders or instructions of the employers. Second, the employee must work within a timetable determined by the employer. Third, the employee must depend economically on the employer, in the sense of deriving his or her livelihood from a regular income paid by the employer. These three elements are not applied mechanically; rather, they allow a court or other authority to have a general picture of the relationship between the worker and the principal, which will be classified as an employer–employee relationship to the extent that it fits into the theoretical category construed by means of the dependency test. If the "dependency" elements result in a relationship which is classified as one between an employer and an employee, this legal status cannot be displaced by a contract or a statement by the parties declaring that a different type of relationship exists. The employer–employee relationship is determined by law and not by the decision of the parties to be governed or not by the rules applicable to such relationship.

Once it is determined that work is performed in the context of an employment relationship, this will have multiple effects on the legal rules applicable to that relationship. With regard to translation work, these effects may be divided into two groups: effects related to work and employment relationships, and effects related to intellectual property.

Regarding the first group of effects, the following may be mentioned:

- The employee will be subject to special limitations on working hours. In developed labour law systems, these limitations are highly complex. Certain rules and maximum working hours are included in the relevant statutes, while additional rules and restrictions may be imposed by collective bargaining agreements. These different rules may impose maximum working hours per day, per week or per month; require additional payments for work exceeding a certain minimum; impose limitations on the period of each day in which work will be performed, particularly during the night; and set special limits on the working hours of women and minors, among other possible rules.
- The employee's compensation will be subject to special rules. If a collective bargaining agreement is applicable, it will set minimum or fixed wage rates and other rules on remuneration, such as payment rates per hours worked in excess of certain levels. These collective bargaining agreement rates, and any other remuneration agreed between the employer and the employee, must comply with more general legal provisions, such as those requiring minimum wages for the country as a whole or for particular regions or activities.
- The employee will be subject to a special social security regime. This may imply withholdings from the employee's remuneration, the obligation to retire after reaching a given age, and the right to retire with a pension once the relevant conditions on age and years of work have been met.
- The employee will be subject to the applicable rules on trade union affiliation and collective bargaining. In some legal systems, these rules imply that the employee can join a given trade union, or one among several trade unions. In other systems, the employee may be bound to the rules included in collective bargaining agreements applicable to the industrial sector where he or she works, even if the employee is not a trade union member. The employee will also be subject to payment of trade union dues, which in some countries are voluntary and in others compulsory even for employees who are not trade union members.
- The employee will be subject to statutory rules on confidentiality, which may be supplemented by agreements with the employer strengthening or clarifying such rules, or imposing additional confidentiality obligations.
- The employee will be subject to instructions by the employer regarding what should be translated and the characteristics of the translation. In a purely contractual relationship, the translator is generally limited by the terms of the relevant contract and by the general rules applicable to

translation, particularly those derived from statutes governing professional translations. An employment relationship places the translator under a much broader set of obligations, since his or her working capacity is placed under the employer's direction. However, the employer's powers in this context are not unlimited. The employee does not have the obligation to comply with unreasonable or illegal instructions. Also, the employer may not force the employee translator to act in violation of the professional rules governing translations, whether statutory or derived from generally accepted practices. In particular, the translator does not have the obligation to comply with instructions which may damage the translator's reputation or professional standing.

- The employee may be subject to statutory non-competition obligations, which may limit the translator's ability to work for other employers or even as an independent translator. The effects of these obligations vary from country to country. In some legal systems, they do not limit the translator's right to do independent work, that is work that does not imply a separate employment relationship, provided that independent work does not interfere with the translator's work for his or her employer and that the product of such work does not compete with the product of the translator's work for his or her employer. In these systems, for example, a translator who is an employee of a law firm and translates legal documents for such law firm may engage in translation work for a publisher of works of fiction, performed after the regular working hours. These non-competition obligations may be extended or limited by means of contractual arrangements between the employer and the employee, but these additional arrangements are subject to legal limits, derived both from competition law and from labour law rules which limit the restrictions that may be imposed on the employee's working capacity.
- Termination of the employment relationship will be subject to special rules. The employee may be under the obligation to provide the employer with advance notice of his or her decision to terminate the employment relationship. Termination by the employer is frequently subject to complex rules. In some countries, such termination is only possible if certain statutory conditions are met. In other legal systems, termination at will requires an additional payment to the employee, generally based on the number of years the employee has worked for the same employer, and this special payment is not applicable if the employer shows that termination is justified due to the employee's breach of his or her statutory or contractual obligations. Termination may be automatic once the employee reaches the age and other conditions necessary for retirement.

5.3 Intellectual property rights in translations produced by employees

Generally, the national legal systems do not have a set of rules applicable to all types of intellectual property in works made by employees. Rather, they include special rules applicable to each type of intellectual property right that may extend to such works. This paragraph will focus on copyright and on the rights on confidential information, since they are the main types of intellectual property right applicable to translations.

Different systems have been adopted with regard to the allocation of copyright in works created by employees. These systems are based on the general rule that the author of a work is the original owner of copyright in that work; the rules on employee-created works operate as exceptions to this general rule.

Under U.S. law, and other similar legal systems, this general rule is modified by provisions which treat the employer as author, with regard to works prepared by an employee within the scope of his or her employment. Section 201(b) of the U.S. Copyright Act provides that:

> The employer or other person for whom the work was prepared is considered the author for purposes of (the Copyright Act), and, unless the parties have expressly agreed otherwise in a written instrument signed by them, owns all of the rights comprised in the copyright.

Hence, when a translation is made by an employee, acting within the scope of his or her employment, copyright will belong to the employer, unless the parties agree otherwise in a written document. The employer is not an assignee but rather the original owner of copyright. "As the legal author of the work, the employer ... owns the copyright free and clear of the inalienable authorship rights which the work's creator would have retained in the case of a mere assignment of copyright" (LaFrance 2008:75).

Applying these provisions requires the determination of whether an employment relationship exists. This has been discussed in 5.2. It also requires defining the limits of the scope of the translator's employment. Not every work or even every translation made by the employee translator will be subject to the rule granting copyright to the employer. A free-lance translation undertaken by the employee during his or her free time will not result in the transfer of copyright to the employer. It will be necessary, in borderline cases, to determine what the actual work of the translator was in the context of his or her employment, so as to decide whether a given translation is part of that work.

Although civil law countries follow rules which are generally similar to those described above, the structure of these rules is somewhat more complex. This additional complexity results, in part, from the frequent lack of a coherent set of rules applicable to the allocation of copyright in works created in the context of employment relationships. It is common, in civil law countries, to have a detailed and complex set of rules applicable to the allocation of patent rights regarding inventions developed by employees. Frequently there is no parallel set of rules in copyright statutes. This is the consequence of the historical development of copyright law. For many decades the author of intellectual works was viewed as a self-employed free-lancer. In fact the development of such works as part of the scope of an author's employment was rather exceptional. This has changed during the last decades, with the rapid growth of the software and entertainment industries, but many countries – particularly in the civil law area – have not kept up in their legislation with these changes. The result is a frequent lack of clear rules on works made for hire, in the copyright statutes. In different countries, several ways have been devised to deal with this statutory vacuum. One possibility is to apply rules included in employment or labour law statutes determining the ownership of intellectual creations generated in the course of employment; either these rules directly apply to copyrightable works or else they refer to other intellectual creations analogous to such works. Another possibility is to apply, by way of analogy, the rules included in patent laws or other intellectual property related statutes. Other countries have inferred solutions to these issues on the basis of more abstract labour law and copyright principles. Under copyright law – in civil law systems – the basic rule is that the individual creator of an intellectual work is the owner of copyright in that work. Employment relationships would provide an exception to this basic rule, since the employee is paid for the work he or she produces within the scope of his or her employment, and property in that work passes to the employer. Hence, work produced within the limits of the creator's employment would belong to the employer, and other works would belong to the employee.

Several civil law countries use three categories of works made in the context of employment to determine copyright in such works. The first group includes works created by employees who have been hired for purposes of creating such works. For example, a translator is hired to translate certain documents necessary for the employer's business. Copyright in works falling into this first group belongs to the employer, although it is possible – though unusual – for the parties to agree otherwise. Generally, there are no special formal requirements for this type of agreement.

A second group includes works created with the occasion of performance of the employee's work or based on information supplied by the employer or obtained in the context of work with that employer. For instance, an engineer working for an industrial company translates certain handbooks written in a foreign language, for purposes of using the translated information in his or her work with such company. Different solutions are possible in these cases. Some legal systems will apply the same solution as for the first category of works, granting copyright to the employer. Other systems follow the same solution, but they require the employer to pay an additional compensation to the employee, based on the premise that the employee was not hired to make this type of work, and that therefore the employer is obtaining a windfall benefit from the employee. Certain countries require the employee to grant a right of first refusal to the employer for the acquisition of copyright. In all these cases, it is possible, but unusual, for the parties to determine the allocation of copyright on this second group of works by means of contracts, although labour law rules will frequently prevent these contracts from extending the employer's rights beyond their original statutory bounds. In other words, these agreements may extend or clarify the employee's original rights, but not limit them.

A third group comprises "independent" creations. These are works which do not fall within the two previously described categories, that is works which are not created with the occasion of performance of the employee's work nor based on information supplied by the employer or obtained in the context of work with that employer. For example, a translation of a novel, made by a translator during his or her free time, such translator generally working as employee for a company engaged in engineering. Copyright in independent creations belongs to the employee. In many legal systems it is not admissible for the parties to agree otherwise, since such an agreement would imply limiting the employee's statutory rights. However, it is possible for the employee to assign or license the rights to specific works, especially after such works have been created, and provided adequate separate consideration is paid to the employee for these assignments or licences.

Applying these three basic categories presents difficulties which must be solved in the context of the applicable national law. In particular, it is necessary to define what is meant by a work created by an employee hired for purposes of creating such work. Normally employees are hired to perform work which is defined vaguely; it is unusual for a translator to be hired for purposes of translating a given book or document. The translator will often be hired to perform translations in general, and it is common for the employee translator to perform, for the same employer, work which does not consist of translation, such as writing documents in a foreign language, or which is unrelated to the translator's linguistic skills, such as paralegal work. To deal with these cases, some countries apply rather restrictive definitions of the type of works which belong to the employees, including only works made by employees hired for purposes of creating such works. Other countries use broader definitions, such as those including works made by an employee in fulfilment of his or her obligations towards the employer in the context of the relevant employment relationship.[2]

Apart from the use of this tripartite classification, civil law systems have

---

[2] See, for example, German Copyright Law, art. 43.

certain rules which differ from those applied in this area by countries such as the United States. In civil law systems, the original author and copyright owner is the individual who, acting as employee, has created the work. Copyright is transferred automatically, as a consequence of a legal provision, and without an express assignment by the author, to the employer, but the author employee remains as the original author of the work, and this has several legal implications. First, in different settings, it may be necessary to identify the individual who is the original author of the work, for purposes of making copyright in that work effective; this may be the case for purposes of copyright registration or of filing court claims based on copyright. Second, the individual author retains the moral rights in the work – these rights have been described in 2.14 above – and this may significantly limit the employer's effective rights in that work, in matters such as the decision to publish such work or the possibility to introduce changes to it.

5.4 Rights in confidential information in the context of employment relationships

Employment relationships create different specific issues related to confidential information. These issues relate to the determination of the rights in valuable confidential information generated by the employee in the context of his or her employment, and to the confidentiality obligations bearing on the employee with regard to the confidential information such employee had access to in the course of his or her employment.

With regard to the first set of issues, they arise due to the fact that employees, during their employment period, may generate trade secrets and other valuable information in the course of their work or in relation thereto. This information may be eventually protected by copyright, patents and other intellectual property rights, in which case the applicable rules will be those related to such rights, displacing the rules governing confidential information. But it is frequently the case that this information, due to its content or to decisions taken by the employer and the employee, is protected by confidentiality, in which case it is necessary to determine who owns the rights in such information.

A set of distinctions similar to that described in connection with copyright – in paragraph 5.3 – is applicable in this area. If the employee was hired with the purpose of generating certain information, that information will belong to the employer. The employee will not have a right to additional compensation in exchange for such information, since the employee's salary is agreed to as payment for this type of work and its information products. A second category includes information based on the tools, information or technology used by the employee in the course of his or her employment, if such information is not generated as part of the employee's obligations towards the employer. Some countries give certain rights to the employer in these cases, such as a right of first refusal to purchase this information or a right to have access and use that information. In these cases, when the employer exercises the relevant rights, the employee commonly may claim a compensation additional to the normal salary, since by hypothesis the employee has completed work, in the employer's benefit, the employee was not hired and paid to perform. A third, residual, category includes information developed by the employee, not included in the first two categories; this information belongs to the employee.

The second set of issues refer to the employee's confidentiality obligations with regard to the information such employee had access to in the course of employment. These obligations are different during the period of employment and after such period. During the employment period, the employee is generally under the obligation to maintain as confidential all the information he or she has access to in the context of his or her work, provided that information, in the context of that work, is kept as confidential by the employer. This last condition does not require an express notice by the employer, regarding every item of confidential information, as to the employee's obligation to keep it confidential or as to the confidential character of the information. The employee is under an obligation to maintain the information as confidential if he or she knew or should have known, in the context of the relevant circumstances, that the information was confidential. For instance, if the employer keeps certain machinery in a room with limited access, the employee must infer that the identity and operation of such machinery is meant to be kept confidential by the employer, and the employees are legally subject to a confidentiality obligation as to that information even in the absence of express agreements to that effect.

After termination of the employment relationship, the former employee is still subject to confidentiality obligations, but these are significantly more limited. The employee is only subject to these obligations with regard to information which objectively is a trade secret; the elements of a trade secret have been described in 4.2 above. If the information was a trade secret at the time employment was terminated, but later loses its trade secret status, the confidentiality obligations disappear. Generally, these confidentiality obligations may be clarified but not extended, since the possibility to use non-secret information acquired in the course of employment is considered necessary for the effectiveness of the employee's right to work with new employers.

5.5 Employer–employee competition

An employer may be interested in preventing an employee from competing in the same business. For example, a firm which hires translators for purposes of organizing translation services for third parties may be interested in preventing the individual translators thus hired from working for other firms, particularly because such employees may thus profit from the commercial knowledge and contacts they have access to in the course of their work.

In some countries labour law includes statutory provisions limiting the employee's right to compete with the employer during the time in which the employment relationship is in place. The employer may release an employee from such restrictions by means of a special permission. After the employment relationship has terminated, the employer may restrict the employees' right to compete with their former employer, by means of a covenant to that effect. These covenants have to comply with different limitations. They must have a reasonable duration – non-compete obligations in excess of five years are generally suspect; they must have a valid reason, such as protecting the former employer's trade secrets; they must have a reasonable geographical scope – a world-wide restriction will be generally considered as excessive; and they must not unduly hinder the employees' possibility to continue working, that is, they may not block the use of the employees' professional capacities.

Other countries only apply restrictions on the employees' competition with the employer if such restrictions result from covenants not to compete. However, in these countries, the employees' competition capacity may in fact be limited by the applicable restrictions on the use of confidential information, described in 5.4 above. Where these covenants not to compete are used, they must comply with standards of fairness and of protection against employer abuse. Under U.S. law, covenants not to compete have to comply with the following criteria: the covenant must protect a legitimate employer interest; the covenant must be no broader than necessary to protect that interest; the covenant must pose no harm to the public interest; and it must present no real hardship for the subject employee (see Rothstein *et al.* 1994:183 v.2).

CASE STUDIES

A. Malcolm, a translator, enters into an agreement with his employer, Dorothy, which includes a provision requiring Malcolm to keep confidential all the information Malcolm has access to during the term of his employment, for a term of five years after termination of such employment. Two years after termination of that employment, part of that information has become public, but Dorothy insists that Malcolm must comply with the confidentiality obligation with regard to all the information received while in Dorothy's employment, regardless of that information's present status. In addition, Dorothy maintains that the confidentiality obligation requires Malcolm not to use that information in the benefit of other employers, even if there is no actual disclosure of the information.

Comments: The prevailing rule in comparative law is that once information becomes public, that is, it is no longer objectively a trade secret, use of that information by a former employee may not be prevented, since that would illegally impinge on such worker's professional capacity. Some countries, however, have adopted a somewhat different approach; they allow confidentiality clauses bearing on former employees if the duration of the confidentiality obligations is similar to the normal duration of the secret character of the information conveyed to the employee, instead of allowing longer confidentiality clauses whose effects terminate upon loss of secrecy. This second approach is to some extent based on judicial expediency rather than on theoretical considerations. Under any of these two systems, a clause providing confidentiality obligations in excess of the admissible limits generally is held not to be completely void, but rather has its duration adjusted to the limits provided by the applicable legal system.

B. Harry works as translator for Engulf Inc., a company engaged in biotechnology. He is specialized in translation of documents related to biotechnology, such as patents and applications for administrative authorizations. During his spare time, Harry translates Chinese poems. A friend of Harry, working in Blue Lotus Inc., a publisher, convinces Harry to publish his translations with Blue Lotus. Harry and Blue Lotus agree to such publication, for which Harry is paid a fixed amount per poem. Engulf finds out about Harry's publications and orders Harry to cease with that line of work, understanding that it is in violation of Harry's non-compete obligations towards Engulf.

Comments: The similarity of Harry's work as an employee and in his free time – in both cases consisting of translation work – does not mean that Harry is competing with his employer or working for a competitor of Engulf. Neither Harry, as a free-lance translator, nor Blue Lotus compete with Engulf since they do not operate in the same markets. Therefore Harry's work for Blue Lotus would not be caught in Harry's non-compete obligations towards Engulf. Engulf could force Harry to enter into an agreement preventing him from this type of activity, but in many legal systems such an agreement would be illegal or unenforceable unless Engulf shows it has a legitimate interest in preventing Harry's out-of-work activities, for example based on the fact that Harry's working capacity under Engulf is affected by his excessive hours of translation work.

C. Lucy does translation work for several clients, including Joyce and Co. After several years of assigning work to Lucy from time to time, in 2001 Joyce increases significantly the frequency with which it assigns translation work to Lucy. By 2005, most of Lucy's work is done for Joyce, and by 2009 Lucy refuses to accept work from other sources, due to her commitments with Joyce. All this time, Lucy does her work from her home, receiving indications, suggestions and corrections, regarding such work, via e-mail. She is paid a fixed amount for each translation, such compensation being negotiated in each case before the work is assigned. In 2011, Joyce abruptly finishes its relations with Lucy, without notice nor apparent motive. Lucy wishes to know whether she has any rights against Joyce.

Comments: Lucy's rights will depend on whether or not she has an employment relationship with Joyce. The existence of an express agreement to that effect has only a secondary value in this matter; an employment relationship will exist legally if certain factual conditions are met, regardless of whether the parties state beforehand that such relationship exists. The relevant factual conditions generally consist of the existence of an economic dependency relationship between the hypothetical employee and his or her employer, the fact that the hypothetical employee works under the command or instructions of the employer, and the fact that the hypothetical employee works during regular hours for the employer. In this case, it is possible, depending on the relevant legal system and the court's criteria, that an employment relationship existed as from 2005 or from 2009. The fact that the employee worked at home has a secondary relevance. If such relationship existed, termination will normally result in several obligations for the employer, such as proving that a proper cause for termination exists – or making an additional severance payment, if such cause is lacking – giving advance notice of the termination, and making a severance payment. In addition, the existence of an employment relationship will generally imply that the employer is subject to special obligations during the employment period, such as paying social security dues and special taxes. Hence, if an employment relationship existed as from 2005 or 2009, and the employer did not comply during the relevant period with the obligations resulting from such relationship, the employer – Joyce and Co. – becomes subject to the liabilities and penalties resulting from that breach.

6. Contracts Related to Translation

6.1 The contractual framework of translation

Translation, as with any other human activity, can be regulated by contract. The general legal rule is that able-minded adults may regulate their legal relationships by means of contracts freely drawn-up and agreed by them. The rules thus agreed to and the obligations resulting therefrom are valid and legally binding, unless a special reason exists to declare their invalidity or lack of effect. For example, a contractual obligation to work for unlimited hours for wages below the legal minimum would be invalid and unenforceable. More generally, a contract or its clauses will be invalid and unenforceable if it violates public policy or is contrary to legal prohibitions or obligations.

Some legal systems identify so-called translation contracts.[1] These are contracts in which one party commissions another to translate a given work, or a number of identified works, specifying the rules that will govern the execution of that translation and payment therefore. These agreements are not regulated in detail by statute, but rather result from long-standing practice and court decisions governing such practice. The general rule applies that the parties may freely determine the contents of these agreements, within the limits described in the preceding paragraph.

There are many other possible types of agreement related to translations. These agreements may govern, for example, the copyright on translations written by several translators; they may be so-called edition contracts, in which the owner of copyright in a translation authorizes its publication and agrees as to its characteristics; they may be agreements between two translators, in which one agrees to oversee and edit the work done by the other. In view of the liberty parties have to regulate by contract their legal relationships, it is not possible to draw an exhaustive list of contracts related to translation. Experience shows that new business and legal environments generate new types of relationship and new types of agreement.

This chapter will describe how contracts are formed and what requirements may be applicable for their full legal effectiveness. It will also describe and analyse the main types of contract related to translations, and their principal provisions.

6.2 Negotiating and entering into an agreement

There are several ways in which an agreement may be negotiated. The "classical" type of negotiation involves two or more parties who discuss the terms of

---

[1] For example, in German law, see Dreier and Schulze (2006:431).

a possible future contract, each of them proposing, discussing and amending the possible provisions of such contract. This type of negotiation is always possible, but it is generally lengthy and costly.

Nowadays, it is more common, even in the area of translations, to enter into an adhesion contract. In these agreements, one of the parties, normally the one with stronger bargaining power, prepares a draft agreement, normally in a pre-established form, which is then submitted for the other party's acceptance. The second party has limited or no possibilities to change the text of the agreement; it is limited to accepting or rejecting the proposed draft.

The legal effects of an adhesion contract are not identical to those of a freely negotiated agreement. "Abusive" clauses imposed by the party proposing the adhesion contract may be considered invalid, and replaced by rules which comply with the applicable legal standards. In some countries, the provisions of some adhesion contracts are subject to special regulatory controls, such as having to be submitted for prior approval by a governmental authority. The standards of interpretation of adhesion contracts are also different, since in case of doubt they are interpreted in favour of the party who accepted the terms imposed by the other.

It is not always possible to determine clearly whether an agreement constitutes an adhesion contract. Adhesion contracts are sometimes executed in a preestablished form, but this is not always the case, and they may be physically indistinguishable from other agreements. Moreover, it may be hard to prove that the agreement was imposed on one of the parties, on a "take it or leave it" basis. Also, the fact that some changes are negotiated regarding a standard agreement does not automatically remove its nature of adhesion contract, which poses the question – without a clear answer – of what degree of negotiations and changes from a proposed text is incompatible with the concept of an adhesion contract.

A third, and more complex, type of negotiation involves several legal steps leading to a final legally binding contract. First, the parties agree by means of a "letter of intent" or a similar document to enter into negotiations leading towards a binding agreement, indicating the basis of such future negotiations and potential agreement. These "letters of intent" may or may not be legally binding – they frequently include language to that effect – but in any case have some legal effects, such as preventing the parties from arbitrarily or abruptly finishing the negotiations. In a second step, the parties may enter into a preliminary agreement, in which they agree to exchange information – for example, about their capabilities, financial situation, past experience and intellectual property rights – define how the negotiations will continue and set out the basic contents of a future definitive agreement. In a third step, if negotiations succeed, a definitive contract is executed. Some of these steps may be omitted, or they may be subdivided into additional stages. This type of complex negotiation is seldom used in the context of agreements with individual translators, and is reserved for negotiations between firms involving lengthy or economically large relationships.

A fourth type of negotiation consists of agreeing to an "umbrella" or basic contract, in which the parties determine, in a legally binding way, the framework of their legal relationships for a relatively long period, leaving certain aspects of such relationships open for negotiation in the context of each individual transaction covered by the basic contract. For example, a publisher and a translator may agree that the translator will work on an unspecified number of translations during a given period and that the parties will agree on the details of the work – time frame, editing, compensation – in connection with each translation.

Legally binding contracts may be entered into in writing or by other means, such as orally or electronically. Unwritten contracts have severe limitations on their validity and effectiveness. In some legal systems they are unenforceable in general or when their purported value exceeds certain amounts. Other legal systems limit the evidence that may be produced to show the existence of the agreement, or only admit such evidence if part of it is in writing or if the parties have begun performing the agreement.

Many countries have special rules for contracts entered into by electronic means. However, these rules frequently require the use of special formalities, such as certification by an authorized authority of the validity and source of the electronic communications involved. If these formalities are not complied with, the legal possibility of using e-mails and other electronic documents as evidence of the agreement may be severely limited.

Written contracts may be entered into by means of a single document or through the exchange of letters or other writings. The simplest mechanism is the execution of a single document by the parties involved. Normally, each party then keeps a copy of the executed contract.

Another possible mechanism is for one of the parties to sign the agreement which is then conveyed to the other party or parties for execution in a different location.

In the case of an exchange of letters, one party sends an offer to the other, including the text of the proposed agreement, and the other responds by accepting the offer. In these cases, the second party may simply accept the initial offer or it may reproduce the text of the agreement.

In all these cases of written agreements, it is possible to ascertain the identity of the parties involved and to minimize future problems as to evidence – for example, regarding the date on which the agreement was signed – through the intervention of a notary public. This is common in civil law countries, but far less so in countries of the Anglo-American legal systems. In civil law countries, the intervention of the notary public may be limited to certifying the identity of the persons executing the agreement, or may extend to registering the agreement in special registries held by the notary public. Some countries require this second form for certain types of agreement, such as those including the assignment of claims subject to litigation.

Contracts may be entered into directly by the parties subject to such contracts or by means of legal representatives. Corporations and other legal entities must act through their legal representatives, such as the president of a corporation, or by means of a person holding a power of attorney. Individuals may also act not only personally but also through their legal representatives – as in the case of minors – or attorneys. Powers of attorney are subject to specific formalities, such as the intervention of a notary public, which vary significantly from country to country.

Some countries also have special recording requirements for certain agreements, particularly those involving copyright. In these cases, the agreement is generally valid even if unrecorded, but has substantial restrictions on its legal effectiveness until registration takes place. For example, a copyright assignment may lack effectiveness against third parties until properly recorded, implying that the assignee cannot sue copyright infringers until recording takes place.

Certain contractual transactions are subject to stamp taxes in some countries. These taxes generally are equivalent to a given percentage of the transaction's value. The contracting party may agree as to how these taxes will be borne. In the absence of payment both parties are jointly liable for the tax and for the penalties that may be applicable.

6.3 Agreements related to translation

It is not possible to draw an exhaustive list of the agreements that may include provisions related to translations. The possibilities run from contracts whose main object is to commission translation work to agreements in which translation is a minor secondary element, such as engineering agreements in which the parties agree that brochures and other written information will be supplied in a given language.

Some legal systems use the expression *translation contracts*, or the equivalent thereof, to refer to agreements in which one party commissions another to translate a given work, or a set of identified works, indicating the rules that will govern such translation and determining the payment therefor. Although many countries do not use this terminology, this type of contract is possible and usual in all legal systems.

As in the case of contracts in general, the parties to translation contracts may determine in detail, in a written contract, the rules that will govern their legal relationships. However, in the absence of such express rules, legal systems include statutory, customary or case-law rules governing the different aspects of these transactions.

By definition, translation contracts must include provisions specifying the work or works to be translated and the rules necessary to determine the identity of such works. For example, a contract may provide that a publisher will select a work each given period – such as a year – which will be presented to the translator. The agreement may set limits to the size of this work and include rules about the time frame and other aspects of the translator's work. Generally, these agreements also include provisions on copyright and on the translator's remuneration. However, as will be described in this chapter, legal systems generally provide rules determining the effects of translation contracts on copyright and the translator's remuneration, applicable in the case of a lack of express provisions in the relevant agreement.

Translation contracts frequently include provisions related to the quality of the translation. In the absence of such provisions, the translator will be subject to the professional standards applicable with relation to the type of translation involved. The translator may be liable for the translation's defects – measured under such standards, and these liabilities may extend even to damages caused to third parties, particularly users of the translation.

Translation agreements may also include provisions on the publication of the translation. From this point of view, translation agreements may become subject to the rules on publication agreements. Many legal systems have special rules applicable to publication agreements, either statutory, customary or developed by case law. Publication agreements create obligations on the author of the work to be published – in this case, a translation – and on the publisher. The author is responsible for the contents and copyright of the work, and the publisher has obligations regarding the time, manner, size, distribution and other aspects of the publication. In some countries, publication agreements must be registered for purposes of copyright protection, and they may be subject to additional formalities, such as the publisher's obligation to deposit a given number of copies of the publication with a governmental agency. Different legal systems have developed a number of miscellaneous rules applicable in the context of publication agreements, which generally may be modified by means of express provisions included by the parties in their agreements. For instance, some laws provide that in case of a new edition of a translated work, the author of the original translation should have preference in relation with other possible translators. Certain legal systems include special rules applicable to the termination of the contractual relationship between the author and the publisher, providing, for instance, that the author has the right to buy from the publisher, with a special discount, the unsold copies remaining from the relevant publication.

It is also possible for a translator to enter into a separate publication agreement, not part of a broader translation contract. For example, a translator may have copyright in a translation of a classic, whose version in the original language is in the public domain. In that case the translator is responsible for his or her representations as to copyright in that translation, and for the delivery of the translation to the publisher. The publisher is responsible for the printing – or electronic setting – of the work, and for its distribution. These agreements generally include detailed provisions regarding different aspects of each party's obligations, such as details about the work to be published, warranties by the translator about the copyright status of that work, provisions regarding the number of copies to be printed and the quality of such copies, obligations as to the distribution of such copies, and rules about termination of the agreement. Agreements of this type frequently include covenants regarding the continuation of publication, providing, for instance, that after a certain number of copies have been sold the publisher will have the option to make additional printings, or indicating that if the work remains out of print for a certain period all rights will revert to the author.

Many countries have special rules applicable to publication agreements, not all of them to be expected by an unaware party. This requires a careful examination of the applicable law, for purposes of determining the effects of this type of agreement. For example, in some countries a publisher of a translation is not allowed to publish a new edition of the same work, translated by a different person, unless the publisher shows the need for such change. Other legal systems include special rules for the termination of the agreement, providing, for instance, that if the publisher's rights have a fixed term, the author has the right to purchase the unsold copies of the work at a preferential price.

A matter which has divergent solutions in comparative law is that of the publisher's rights in case of copyright violation. The typical facts in this type of case are the following. A publisher prints and distributes a book with the author's authorization. An unauthorized party publishes the same book, damaging the publisher's sales. All legal systems grant the author rights to stop this unauthorized publication. However, the publisher does not have similar rights under basic copyright law. The publisher is not the copyright owner, but only a licensee of the author or of the copyright owner. The author may not be interested in acting against the infringer. For example, the author may derive no additional compensation from sales by the publisher – as will be the case if the author received a fixed amount for the licence – or may be more interested in additional sales than in payments from the publisher, or may be in a situation of conflict or enmity with the publisher, or – finally – may have ideological reasons not to act against infringers. This situation places the publisher in a position of clear competitive disadvantage, since he or she must then compete in the same markets with publishers who make no payments for copyright.

The different national legal systems, and the contractual practice developed thereunder, have devised several solutions for this situation. In some countries, the publisher has a special right to act against unauthorized copies of the works published by the publisher. This is a type of so-called neighbouring right, granted directly to the publisher, and which does not depend on the author's action; the author has separate claims for copyright violation. In other countries, a publisher having an exclusive licence from the author may have the right to file claims for copyright infringement, while other legal systems allow the publisher, in these cases, to act against the infringer on the basis of the latter's unfair competition. Another solution – in this case resulting from contractual clauses to that effect – is for the author to assign his or her copyright to the publisher, who is then legally empowered to file legal actions against copyright infringers. In other cases, the publisher obtains a power of attorney from the author, allowing such publisher to file complaints, in the name of the author, against copyright infringers.

6.4 Contractual provisions on payment for translation work

Translation work is normally performed, in the benefit of parties other than the translator, in exchange for a valuable consideration. This is not only a fact derived from common experience, but also the basis of legal provisions based on that fact. Translation work – as with other types of work and service – is not deemed to be gratuitous unless there is a strong legal reason – such as an express contractual provision – to conclude that no consideration is payable for that work.

Normally, agreements related to translation specify the payments to be made for the translator's work. There are many possible and valid legal mechanisms to determine the amount of such payments. In some cases a fixed amount is agreed for the whole work, while in others payments are calculated on the basis of a given unit, such as translated words, or pages of translation. It is also possible for the translator to work on the basis of hours of work, the parties agreeing on an hourly rate; this mechanism may be especially appropriate when the translator works in the commissioning party's premises or under such party's direct supervision.

The parties are not totally free to negotiate the payments due for translation work. If the translator has an employment relationship with the party paying for the translation, payments must comply with the applicable labour law rules, which may provide a minimum payment per hour, per day or per week, as well as compulsory rules about how the remuneration must be calculated. These rules may refer to the way the hours of work are calculated – for example, including or not the time spent moving to and from the place or work; they may provide additional payments if the employee works more than a given number of hours in a certain day or in another relevant period; they may require special payments during periods of sickness, vacation, pregnancy or other situations preventing the employee from working normally; and may govern many other aspects of the employee's remuneration, such as the periodicity and form of payment.

Another set of restrictions on the negotiation of payments due for translations may result from special legal and regulatory rules applicable to translators. These rules may apply regardless of whether the translator works as an employee or not. These rules may provide fixed or minimum rates – hourly, per word, or on other bases – for translations, with variations depending on the language, whether the translator certifies or not the accuracy of the translation, and other variables. These rules may result directly from statutes, or may be issued by translators' associations or other institutions with legal powers to determine fixed or minimum rates.

It is not uncommon for translators to be hired for translation work without a prior agreement as to the applicable consideration for such work. In most of these cases the parties reach an agreement about payment during the course of such work or after it is delivered, and such agreement is valid within the limits described above for agreements on translators' remuneration. However, sometimes an agreement of this type is not possible, and it becomes necessary to determine the rules which will apply to calculate such remuneration, in the context of litigation or before that stage is reached.

A basic rule is that the translator's work must be paid, even in the absence of prior agreement, unless – as has been described above in this paragraph – there are reasons to conclude that the parties had agreed that the translation was free of charge. It should be noted that if the translator already is paid – particularly, as an employee – to do translation work, he or she is not working gratuitously, and payments in addition to the translator's salary or current payment will not be due unless the translator can show that a given translation was beyond the scope of the work for which he or she receives a salary or current payment.

Once it has been determined that payment for a given translation has to be established, there are several ways to determine the amount of such payment in the absence of agreement between the parties. In some countries, there are statutory rules which directly or indirectly – in this case, through regulations and other provisions issued by translators' associations and other institutions – determine the translator's remuneration. Other legal systems have statutory or case-law rules providing that, in the absence of a prior agreement about the value of a service – in this case, a translation – such value shall be determined according to normal market practices. The enforcement of these rules will require evidence about the current rates for translation work, and these rates will be applicable.

A special case is that of the remuneration of translators doing work in the context of judicial and other procedures. The law in this area is highly variable from one jurisdiction to another. Generally, there are certain types of translation regarding which the parties are free to hire translators and to negotiate the applicable fees according to the contractual rules described in this paragraph. This is the case, for example, with the translation of foreign language documents to be presented in court. But there are other types of translation for which translators are appointed by the court; for instance, an interpreter may be appointed in the context of a deposition by a person who cannot speak the language of the court, or a translator may be designated to translate a foreign law that must be applied by the court. In these cases, some legal systems have official schedules determining the translators' fees, on bases such as the hours worked or the number of words translated. However, these schedules, or the courts' decisions determining the translators' fees on the basis of such schedules may also take into account the value of the litigation or process in the context of which the translation is performed.

Certain issues may arise in connection with the payment for translations when the payor and the payee are located in different countries. Some countries place restrictions on the purchase of foreign exchange or on payments to persons located abroad, and this may limit the possibility of forwarding payments to a translator working in other jurisdictions. In addition, many countries impose withholding taxes on payments made to persons outside their territories. These withholdings generally constitute a mechanism to make effective the income taxes applicable on the relevant payments. Generally, these withholdings are calculated on the basis of a flat rate, which may vary depending on the type of income involved. For instance, a different rate may be applicable on royalties payable for the use of works protected by copyright and on payments for translation work not covered by copyright. In many cases, these withholdings may be used in the translator's home country as a credit against taxes due in such country. Also, there are many bilateral or multilateral treaties which may govern these taxes when the translator and the payor are located in specific countries.

6.5 Copyright in the context of contracts related to translation

If a translator authors a translation in the context of a translation contract or of another contractual relationship, it is necessary to determine ownership of the copyright in the resulting translation. As in other legal areas, there are fundamental differences in the approach used by civil law countries and legal systems of the Anglo-American tradition, although the final results are not radically different.

In civil law countries, the premise on which the applicable rules are based is that the translator, as the individual who has authored the translation, is the original owner of copyright in that translation. Therefore, for another party to claim ownership of such copyright there must be a legal relationship pursuant to which copyright is transferred. Such relationship may be an express contractual provision transferring copyright to the person who commissioned the translation, or to another party identified in the relevant contract, or a contractual relationship from which a similar transfer is inferred. This will generally be the case if the translator is paid for carrying out the translation.

These copyright transfers, taking place in the context of civil law systems, are limited to the author's economic or exploitation rights – described in 2.13 above – and not to moral rights – described in 2.14.

Under U.S. law, the category of *works made for hire* includes not only works prepared by employees but also certain works specially ordered or commissioned. Translations are included among these works (U.S Copyright Act, Section 101). On the basis of these rules, works created by independent contractors qualify as works made for hire, provided the parties "expressly agree in a written instrument signed by them that the work shall be considered a work made for hire". Copyright in these works belongs to the person who commissioned the relevant work.

In these different legal systems, it is possible to include additional provisions on copyright and other intellectual property rights in the contracts linking a translator with other parties. The parties may expressly determine the property rights in the works generated in the context of their legal relationships, instead of allowing such rights to be assigned on the basis of the categorization of their relationships as "hiring", "rendering of services", or other concepts used by the applicable law to determine the original copyright owner. For example, they may agree that, even if a work is made for hire, copyright will belong to the author, and the person commissioning such work will only have certain rights to use it in a limited time period or business scope. However, these contractual provisions are subject to multiple limitations.

In civil law systems, moral rights are retained by the author, regardless of what the parties may agree to contractually. Hence, an assignee of copyright by virtue of a contractual clause only acquires economic or exploitation rights, and may require the author's permission for transactions such as updating or otherwise changing the original work. These limitations are more flexible in countries of the Anglo-American legal system.

Also, contractual provisions imposed on translators – as with other authors – without proper negotiation, as is the case in the context of adhesion contracts (see par 6.2 above), may be deemed abusive and unenforceable.

Contractual clauses may also be considered invalid – even if resulting from a fully negotiated transaction – if they improperly interfere with the author's working capacity or livelihood. For example, an agreement in which an author agrees to assign copyright on all her or his future work, without additional consideration, deprives such author from the incentives provided by copyright to intellectual work, and may be considered illegal or unenforceable.

Agreements related to translation may include provisions assigning or licensing the translator's copyright. These provisions are applicable when, pursuant to the rules governing the translator's work, such translator is the copyright owner regarding such work. The translator may agree to assign the copyright to the party commissioning the work or to another party mentioned in the agreement, or to grant a licence to any of these parties. In the case of an assignment, the result is not identical to that applicable in cases in which the party paying for the work is the original owner of the copyright; the fact that the translator is the original owner and that copyright is assigned may have multiple consequences on the applicable protection, in connection with matters such as the duration of the copyright protection and the tax rules applicable to the proceeds received by the author. The translator may also agree to grant a licence allowing the party commissioning the work the possibility of reproducing or otherwise exploiting the work, within the limits provided by the agreement, but keeping the intellectual property rights in the translator's possession.

6.6 Breach of contract

The legal significance of contracts would be very limited in the absence of remedies applicable in the case of breach of contract. These remedies are different in the various legal systems. Their effectiveness must be assessed in the context of the particular circumstances of each case. A slow court system or an insolvent debtor may render a contract practically useless.

The applicable statutory or case law includes rules for cases of breach of contract. In addition, the parties may include provisions in their contracts addressing the consequences of such breach.

There are certain consequences of breach of contract which are common to most legal systems. An immediate possibility is the action for specific performance, in which a party requests an order enjoining the breaching party to perform its obligations as agreed in a contract. Civil law systems generally consider that this is a necessary legal consequence of contractual breach. The Anglo-American legal system was traditionally more restrictive towards this type of action, generally preferring the payment of damages as compensation to be paid by the party in breach of contract.

Even in civil law systems, specific performance may be impossible in many cases. A person who must render certain services or generate a work personally may not be forced physically to act as agreed. This is particularly the case with translations. If a person has agreed to translate a literary work, such person may not be physically coerced to undertake such translation.

If it is not legally or practically possible to obtain specific performance of a contractual obligation, an alternative remedy may consist in obtaining performance of the agreed and breached obligation by a third party, at the breaching party's cost. Although statutory and case law frequently provide this alternative, it is not always practically viable. In many cases, especially those including intellectual work, there is a personal element in the performance of obligations, which cannot be fully replaced by a third party. For example, if a prestigious translator is hired to translate a famous literary work, his services cannot be satisfactorily substituted by those of another translator.

The party whose contractual rights have been breached may request, if such breach has not been redressed by specific or third-party performance, the payment of damages. Calculation of such damages is complex and varies between the different national legal systems. Generally, damages are calculated so that the injured party is placed in a position which is not worse than that which would have existed in the absence of the contractual breach. This will normally require the return to the damaged party of monies and other payments made to the breaching party, the compensation of losses incurred by the damaged party, and an additional amount reflecting the profits the damaged party would have normally obtained if the contract had been properly performed.

When the contractual obligation to be performed consists in the payment of money – for example, payment of the price agreed for a translation – lack of payment at the agreed time will result in an additional obligation to pay interest on the amount owed, until payment is made. This interest may be determined in the relevant contract or may be imposed by a court on the basis of the applicable statutory or case law provisions.

Another consequence of the breach of one party's obligations is that such breach allows the other party to delay or stop performance of its own obligations. This characteristic or element of contractual obligations is sometimes named *constructive conditions of exchange*, although it is identified in civil law countries by the Latin expression *exceptio non adimpleti contractus*, meaning that one party may oppose as exception to performance of its contractual obligations the fact that the other party has not complied with its own obligations. The detailed application of these principles is complex and varies from country to country. It requires a clear determination of the time in which each party must perform its contractual obligations, since only after such time has expired is it possible to argue that such party is in default and that the other party may consequently suspend performance of its own obligations.

A more drastic effect of breach of contract is that the party which is not guilty of such breach may terminate the agreement. This will be discussed in paragraph 6.7.

In addition to the legal consequences and remedies resulting from breach of contract, the parties may include provisions in their agreement extending or limiting such consequences and remedies. Common contractual provisions related to these matters include so called penalty clauses and liquidated damages clauses. Penalty clauses provide that an infringing party must pay a penalty to the other party. Depending on the text of the clause and the applicable legal provisions, a penalty clause may or may not replace the non-infringing party's right to damages, and may or may not do away with the infringing party's obligation to perform the terms agreed in the contract. For example, a penalty clause may provide that if a translator does not deliver a given translation by day X, such translator will owe a penalty equivalent to Y, and will still bear the obligation to deliver the translation at a later date. Liquidated damages clauses provide that if a non-infringing party has the right to recover damages from the party in default, such damages shall be calculated as provided in such clauses.

Penalty and liquidated damages clauses are useful and common in contracts related to services and intellectual property. It is difficult in these cases to force compliance with the party who must perform services and also to calculate the damages caused by non-performance. Let us imagine the case of a publisher A who hires a prestigious translator B, as part of a project involving the translation of famous modern literary works. If B refuses to complete the translation, A cannot physically force B to undertake it. A replacement for B may be able to carry out the translation, but without the same quality level – an aspect which is hard to measure by a court – and without the reputation value of B's work. In addition, the fact that B does not participate in the project may damage its overall prestige and may undermine A's marketing efforts. All these factors are difficult to specify conceptually and even more difficult to quantify precisely in the context of a legal procedure. A penalty or liquidated damage clause may allow the plaintiff to overcome these difficulties and save costly legal procedures when trying to redress a contractual breach.

However, penalty and liquidated damages are not without theoretical and practical limitations. They become unenforceable or subject to modification by the court if they are abusive, particularly if payments under these clauses clearly exceed the real damages suffered by the plaintiff. They are particularly suspect if included in adhesion contracts – described in 6.2 above – or in contracts with consumers.

6.7 Contract termination

The termination of contracts is subject to special rules, many of which have relatively unexpected consequences from a layman's point of view. Much of the litigation related to contracts – and specifically to contracts related to translation – is related to their termination.

The basic rule is that the parties may include in their agreements the rules that will govern their termination. It is common, especially in complex transactions, to include a basic rule providing the duration of the agreement. These provisions may establish a duration counted as from a certain date, such as the execution date of the agreement, or they may provide that the agreement will expire on a given date. Frequently, they will also include rules for the renewal of the agreement. For example, they may provide that the agreement will be extended for additional periods, either because the parties agree to do so in writing or by other means, or because the agreement is deemed extended if none of the parties declares its will to the contrary within a given period. In addition, this type of agreement includes additional termination clauses, listing certain circumstances which will result in the automatic termination of the agreement, or which allow one of the parties to terminate the agreement by means of a unilateral statement. These termination clauses are highly variable. Typically they allow termination if one of the parties defaults on its obligations and does not cure such default within a given period, or if one of the parties dies – particularly, authors – or is liquidated – in the case of legal entities – or becomes subject to insolvency procedures. Under some contracts termination may be decided by one of the parties if certain objective conditions take place, such as sales of a given book being under a specified figure, or a commissioning party not being selected by a third party to perform certain work. The parties are generally free to agree on whatever termination provision they deem fit.

There are, however, several types of legal restrictions on the validity and effects of termination provisions. In some legal systems, certain causes of contract termination are considered invalid. This is the case, particularly, with termination based on the bankruptcy of one of the parties. In these legal systems, if a party to a contract falls into bankruptcy, such contract becomes subject to special statutory provisions, and the parties are not free to decide by themselves whether to terminate it or not. Also, termination clauses may be illegal if they are a mechanism to impose illegal constraints on one of the parties, for example, if termination is provided on the basis of one of the parties' religious or political preferences, or in cases in which a provider of services does not comply with a work schedule which exceeds the acceptable legal limits.

Termination at will, even when accepted without limitations in a contractual provision, may be subject to restrictions. Especially in the case of long-term contracts, the party deciding the termination may be under the obligation to indicate its desire to finish the agreement a reasonable number of days before termination becomes effective. That number is variable and may depend on the circumstances of each case: duration of the previous relationship between the parties, the difficulties such parties may experience in readjusting their work, and the reasons for the termination. Also, statutory or case law may require, in this type of contract, a valid reason for the termination, and while such termination may still be effective in the absence of a valid reason, the party deciding the termination may be liable for damages.

If a contract creates an employment relationship, the rules on termination may be far more complex and restrictive of the parties' freedom to terminate the contract at will. In many countries, the party terminating an employment relationship must give advance notice of the termination, or pay an amount to compensate for an eventual lack of prior notice. If termination is decided by the employer, it may be possible only if a proper cause is shown, or may be subject to stringent indemnification provisions – often based on the employee's seniority – if no such cause exists.

If no termination provisions are included in the agreement, contract law provides rules governing termination. If a specific duration may be implied from the terms of the agreement, it will be applicable in a way similar to an express duration provision. This is the case, for example, when the wording or context of the agreement leads to the conclusion that it was entered into for a specific translation; once such translation is completed, the agreement finishes, as if such termination cause had been agreed by the parties.

If an agreement has no express termination provisions and no implied duration term can be implied from its wording, generally any of the parties can terminate the agreement by notifying the other party of its intent to finish the contractual relationship. Not including a clear termination provision does not result in an agreement which cannot be terminated, but rather in a contract that any of the parties can terminate at will. However, the exercise of this termination should not be abusive. In particular, reasonable prior notice should be given by the party wishing to terminate the transaction. The reasonable length of the term between the day of the notice and the moment in which the contract should expire should contemplate aspects such as the possibility of replacing that agreement with a different contract with a third party, the length of the period during which the agreement had been in effect – the longer such period, the longer the required term between notice and termination – and the difficulties the parties may experience in adjusting their conduct to the proposed termination.

Termination of a contract may result in several specific obligations for the parties. There may be contractual restrictions on work for other parties or on other competing activities. The parties may have the obligation to return materials received during the course of the agreement, or not to use them; this may be the case, for example, with software supplied by one of the parties for purposes of the other party's performance.

6.8 Dispute resolution

Contractual transactions may result in disputes between the parties. The legal rules applicable to such transactions provide the framework within which such disputes must be solved. However, the enforcement of such rules may be complex, lengthy and costly. Providing adequate dispute resolution mechanisms may be as practically important as agreeing about the rules that will govern the substance of these disputes.

It is possible not to include any provisions on dispute resolution in the text of a contract. In that case, the relevant legal systems provide the rules applicable to such dispute resolution. Each legal system has its own rules about the reach of its jurisdiction, the applicable procedures, the time frame within which litigation must take place and other aspects of procedure and litigation.

With regard to jurisdiction, the different legal systems have very diverse rules on the determination of the courts having the power to decide a case. These rules vary depending on the type of case involved. For example, if an action is brought based on a contract violation, jurisdiction may be determined on the base of the defendant's domicile, or of the location of the contract's performance or of other factors. The plaintiff may have a choice between different alternative venues. In many legal systems, courts have not only territorial limits on their jurisdiction, but also limits on the type of cases they may hear. Therefore, depending on the type of case involved, the plaintiff may be constrained to sue before a certain type of court, for example, a small claims court, or a court for civil cases.

The parties may include in their contracts provisions on jurisdiction and dispute resolution. Typically, they may include a clause providing that any disputes related to the relevant contract will be subject to a specific jurisdiction, for example, the commercial courts of a given city. These clauses may provide an exclusive jurisdiction – implying that no other jurisdiction, other than that chosen by the parties, may act in cases related to the contract – or one or more possible jurisdictions, without preventing the parties from acting as plaintiffs in other jurisdictions which may be open to their claims.

There are limitations on the jurisdictions that may be chosen contractually by the parties. Generally, clauses on choice of jurisdiction are valid, but the chosen jurisdiction must have a relevant relationship with the dispute, such as acting in the location where one of the parties has its domicile or where the contract is performed. The validity of these clauses may be severely limited in the case of contracts involving consumers or in adhesion contracts (see paragraph 6.2 above). In these types of contracts, the choice of a jurisdiction which is inconvenient or costly for the consumer or for the party accepting the adhesion contract may be considered an abusive clause. The choice will be disregarded and jurisdiction will be determined as if the clause did not exist.

The parties may submit their conflict to alternative dispute resolution mechanisms. This may take place by means of a clause included in a contract or, even in the absence of such a clause, if the parties agree to use such mechanisms after the dispute has arisen. In some countries it is compulsory to submit certain disputes to alternative dispute resolution mechanisms, particularly mediation, before a complaint is filed with a court.

The main alternative dispute resolution mechanisms are mediation and arbitration. In the case of mediation, a third party, chosen by the parties in the contract or thereafter, tries to facilitate an agreement between the parties as to the matter in dispute. Mediators normally are individuals specialized in dispute resolution and with knowledge of the legal field in which the dispute has arisen. If mediation is required before cases are brought to court, mediators must be chosen from an official list. Mediators do not have the power to decide the case. They may recommend solutions, and if no agreement is reached by the parties, the dispute becomes open for litigation. Contractual clauses or the applicable legal provisions may include a minimum period during which mediation must be tried and in which litigation is temporarily barred.

Arbitration takes place before one or more arbitrators, who have the power to decide a legal dispute. Contractual clauses may submit disputes to arbitration, either in broad terms, or specifying the rules that will be applicable to the arbitration. These clauses may be limited to a provision stating that disputes between the parties will be submitted to arbitration, in which case there are procedural rules which will govern the arbitration. These rules provide how the arbitrator is selected, the procedural rules applicable to the arbitration and other aspects necessary for the arbitration clause to be effective. The contractual arbitration clauses may also be limited to selecting one of the many arbitration systems available, for example, that of the International Chamber of Commerce. If this type of selection is made, the arbitration system will include rules on the selection of arbitrators and on the applicable procedure. Arbitration clauses may also be more detailed, including in their terms the selection of arbitrators and the rules applicable during the arbitration.

Depending on the terms of the arbitration clause, the dispute may be decided by the arbitrators on the basis of the legal provisions applicable to such dispute or on the basis of equity, fairness or other not strictly legal standards.

Arbitration has several advantages and disadvantages. Its convenience depends on the circumstances of each case. Arbitration is normally faster than judicial litigation. However, arbitrators do not have the legal powers of judges, and this may limit its effectiveness. For example, arbitrators may be forced to act through the courts to obtain evidence. Also, if the parties refuse to comply with an arbitration award, it may be necessary to enforce it through the courts, and this may lead to protracted litigation. In terms of costs, arbitration may be free of some of the expenses which are associated, in some countries, with litigation, such as court taxes, stamp taxes and compulsory legal fees. But arbitration frequently requires specialized legal expertise, with its corresponding cost.

CASE STUDIES

A. Joao Dos Santos, a Brazilian translator, agrees in a meeting with a publisher to translate a book from French into Portuguese. No payment terms are discussed in the meeting and no written agreement is entered into. Several months after the meeting, Joao starts sending chapters of the translation to the publisher. After five chapters – more than half of the whole book – have been sent to the publisher, Joao receives a letter in which the publisher "rejects" the translation, stating that the publisher "does not accept the quality of the work". Joao wishes to know what his rights are against the publisher.

Comments: There are generally legal restrictions on actions brought on the basis of agreements not entered into in writing, and on the evidence that may be offered to show the existence of such agreements. However, most legal systems allow claims based on contracts not executed in writing if the parties have started performance of such agreements. If such performance exists, these legal systems allow evidence showing that there was an unwritten agreement which is being performed. In this type of case, it is necessary to show that performance was not unilaterally decided by the performing party; one party cannot "enter" into an agreement simply by beginning its performance. In the case of Joao's translation, the fact that the publisher receives several chapters without immediately rejecting them and that rejection is afterwards based on "the quality of the work" would suggest that the translation had been originally commissioned by the publisher and that it was subject to the publisher's quality standards. Joao would then be able to introduce evidence, in a possible litigation, about the existence of an unwritten contract. If no quality standards or payment conditions were agreed, the normal standards and payments prevailing for similar translations would generally be applicable.

B. Jenkinson, a lawyer, hires Poots, on February 1st, to translate a legal document. The translation must be filed in court on February 7th. On February 6th, Poots notifies Jenkinson that he cannot deliver the translation by February 7th, "due to previously unforeseen circumstances". Jenkinson then contacts Champion, a famous professor, to do the translation. Champion agrees to finish the translation by the due time, but at a price of ten thousand dollars. Jenkinson agrees to pay that price. Champion delivers the translation in time and is paid the agreed amount. Jenkinson then sues Poots to recover the cost of having the document translated by a third party, Champion.

Comments: Non-performance of contractual obligations may be excused by unforeseen circumstances which prevent the obligor from performing such obligations. However, the obligor subject to such circumstances must act with proper diligence so as not to cause unnecessary hardships or costs to the other contractual party. In this case, Poots's conduct does not appear to comply with proper diligence standards. Notice of Poots's difficulties was given shortly before expiration of the time in which the translation work was due, and there is no apparent reason for this short notice which places Jenkinson in a very difficult position. Generally, a party in Jenkinson's position has the right to obtain performance by a third party of an obligation which the obligor has declared he will not perform. But this right must be exercised reasonably, so as to mitigate the damages caused by the obligor's default. In this case, Jenkinson may have difficulties in transferring to Poots the full cost of the translation unless Jenkinson can show that she had no alternative to commissioning Champion.

C. Mercier, who lives in France, does part-time work as translator for Consolidated Everything, Inc. After several years of working on and off for Consolidated, Mercier receives an e-mail stating that in the future her relationship with Consolidated shall take place under an agreement to be signed in the next three days. Mercier receives an agreement form. She doesn't agree with some of its terms, but after a mild objection made to an officer of Consolidated she is told that this is a "take it or leave it" contract, and that if she doesn't sign it she will no longer receive work from Consolidated. Mercier signs the agreement. It includes a provision stating that all disputes related to the agreement will be subject to arbitration and that such arbitration shall take place in New York. For a few years relations between Mercier and Consolidated remain cordial. However, Consolidated is acquired by a conglomerate. Less work is given to Mercier, and one day she is told that a major transaction was lost due to a delay in the delivery of a translation she had been commissioned to complete. Consolidated starts arbitration proceedings in New York to recover damages from Mercier. Mercier does not have the resources to defend herself. She loses the arbitration and Consolidated is now enforcing the award in France.

Comments: The agreement between Mercier and Consolidated is an adhesion contract. Abusive clauses included in such an agreement, imposing undue hardship on the party accepting the agreement, are unenforceable or invalid, depending on the applicable legal system. Clauses changing the applicable jurisdiction and making the legal defence of the "weak" party more costly are among those that are commonly considered abusive. Consolidated obtained a favourable award but needs to enforce it in France, where Mercier has assets. Enforcement of foreign awards is made through a special procedure which generally requires a determination by the enforcing court to the effect that the award being enforced does not violate the law of the enforcing jurisdiction. The fact that Mercier's legal position was substantially weakened by the practical impossibility of litigating in New York may result in the unenforceability of the award.

Bibliography

Bellos, David (2011) *Is That a Fish in Your Ear? Translation and the meaning of everything*, New York: Faber & Faber.
Bently, Lionel (1993) 'Copyright and Translations in the English Speaking World', *Translatio*, XII:4, 491–559.
Born, Gary B. (1996) *International Civil Litigation in United States Courts,* The Hague: Kluwer Law International.
Chesterton, Gilbert Keith (2011) 'The Great Victorian Poets' in Ian Ker (ed.) *The Everyman Chesterton,* New York: Alfred A. Knopf, 255–277.
Correa, Carlos M. (2007) *Trade Related Aspects of Intellectual Property Rights,* Oxford: Oxford University Press.
David, René and John Brierley (1985) *Major Legal Systems in the World Today: An introduction to the comparative study of law*, London: Stevens.
Dessemontet, François (1976) *The Legal Protection of Know-how in the United States*, Geneva: F.B. Rothman.
----- (1999) *Le droit d'auteur,* Lausanne: CEDIDAC.
Dreier, Thomas and Gernot Schulze (2006) *Urheberrechtsgesetz,* Munich: C.H.Beck.
Emery, Miguel Ángel (1999) *Propiedad intelectual*, Buenos Aires: Astrea.
Fawcett, James and Paul Torremans (1998) *Intellectual Property and Private International Law*, Oxford: Clarendon Press.
Fawcett, James, Janeen Carruthers and Peter North (2008) *Cheshire, North & Fawcett: Private International Law,* Oxford: Oxford University Press.
Geller, Paul Edward (2011) *International Copyright Law and Practice*, New York: LexisNexis.
Hay, Peter, Patrick J. Borchers and Symeon Symeonides (2010) *Conflict of Laws,* Saint Paul, MN: West.
LaFrance, Mary (2008) *Copyright Law,* Saint Paul, MN: Thomson/West.
Leaffer, Marshall (1995) *Understanding Copyright Law*, New York: Matthew Bender.
Lipszyc, Delia (1993) *Derechos de autor y derechos conexos,* Buenos Aires: UNESCO, CERLALC, Zavalía.
MacLaren, Terrence F. (1997) *Worldwide Trade Secrets Law,* Deerfield, Illinois: Clark Boardman Callaghan.
Nimmer, Melville and David Nimmer (1997) *Nimmer on Copyright,* Albany: Matthew Bender.
Phillips, Jeremy, Robyn Durie and Royce Whale (1997) *Whale on Copyright,* London: Sweet and Maxwell.
Reimann, Mathias and Reinhard Zimmermann (2008) *The Oxford Handbook of Comparative Law*, Oxford: Oxford University Press.
Rothstein, Mark A., Charles B. Craver, Elinor P. Schroeder, Elaine Shoben and Lea S. VanderVelde (1994) *Employment Law*, Saint Paul, MN: West.

Venuti, Lawrence (1995a) *The Translator's Invisibility: A history of translation*, New York, Routledge.
----- (1995b) 'Translation, Authorship, Copyright', *The Translator* 1(1): 1–24.
World Intellectual Property Organization (1988) *Background Reading Materials on Intellectual Property*, Geneva: WIPO.

Index

Abusive clauses 115, 126, 132
Acceptance 116
Adaptation rights 37
Adaptations 26, 52, 53, 56, 59
Adhesion contracts 12, 115, 123, 126, 129, 132
Administrative procedures 11
Advance notice 127
Alternative dispute resolution 129
Anglo-American legal systems 3, 4, 17, 29, 43, 48, 81, 91, 92, 101, 102, 116, 122–124
Anonymous works 30, 40
Anthologies 26, 30
Applicable law 5
Arbitration 9, 10, 129, 130
Arbitration clauses 129, 130, 132
Archives 43
Artistic works 23
Assignments 32–33, 60, 69, 75, 79, 108, 109, 117, 120, 123
Audiovisual works 23, 34
Authorization to translate 67–69
Authorship 64–66, 106

Bankruptcy 127
Berne Convention 14, 16–19, 24–30, 32, 35–50, 52, 53, 58, 67, 70–72
Breach of confidence 91
Breach of confidentiality rules 99
Breach of contract 124–126, 131
Breach of duty 91
Broadcasting organizations 45, 45
Business secrets 78, 84

Case law 4
Certification 11
Choice 65, 66
Choice of law 6, 7, 9
Cinematographic works 23, 26, 27, 30, 32, 36, 39, 40
Civil law systems 3, 4, 17, 29, 43, 81, 91, 92, 101–103, 106, 107, 109, 116, 122–124
Civil remedies 44, 81
Classified information 76, 98

Collaboration 30
Collections 26, 30
Collective bargaining agreements 104
Collective works 30–32, 63
Commercial information 89
Common knowledge 95, 100
Communication rights 37
Competition 110
Composite works 31, 32, 63
Computer-assisted works 64–66
Computer-generated works 64–66
Computer programs *see* software
Confidential information 76–100, 110
Confidentiality 15, 76–100, 104, 106, 109–112
Confidentiality agreements 84, 87–89, 93, 99
Conflict of laws 6, 9, 13
Conflicts 1, 2
Consideration 120
Constitutional rights 88, 99
Constructive conditions of exchange 125
Contract law 87–89, 114–132
Contract termination 126–128
Contractors 89
Contracts 1, 87–89, 93
Contracts related to translation 114–132
Contractual clauses 93, 96, 111, 112, 123
Contractual negotiations 114, 115
Contractual relationships 84, 94
Control test 102
Cooperation 30
Copyright 14–51, 106–109, 118, 119, 122–124
Copyright in translations 67–70
Copyright protection of translations 52–75
Copyright violation 61
Corporate directors 85
Corporate relationships 85
Court translators 94, 121
Creativity 20, 24, 55–58, 64
Criminal penalties 44, 45, 81, 86, 87

Damages 44, 92, 99, 125, 127
Data compilations 24, 26, 49
Dead authors 72
Dependency 103, 113
Derivative works 21, 22, 62, 67, 68, 70
Developing countries 72
Dispute resolution 50, 128–130
Droit de suite 37
Duration 126
Duress 83

Economic rights 33, 35–40, 59, 60, 123
Edition contracts 114
Educational use 41, 42
Electronic agreements 116
Employees 32, 82, 83, 86–88, 92, 93, 101–113
Employers 32, 82, 83, 92, 93, 101–113
Employment 82, 83, 87, 88, 92, 93, 99–113, 120, 127
Employment contract 102, 103
Enforcement 8, 9, 10, 49, 50, 132
Enforcement of awards 132
Ethics 11
European Union 5, 16, 26
Evidence 28, 97, 98, 130, 131
Exceptions from copyright in translation 70–72
Excluded works 24, 25
Exclusive jurisdiction 129
Exclusive licences 34
Exclusive rights 18, 34, 35
Exclusivity 75
Exemptions from copyright protection 40–43, 70–72
Exhaustion 42
Experts 12
Exploitation rights 33, 35–38, 59, 60, 68, 73
Expression 19, 24, 51, 54, 57

Fair use 40–43, 60, 71
Fee schedules 122
Fees 11, 121,122
Films 23, 26, 27
First sale 42
Fixation 20, 27, 45
Folklore 26
Foreign judgments 9

Formal requirements 27, 28, 47
Fraud 83
Functional aspects 51

Honest commercial practices 80

Ideas 19, 24, 51, 54, 57
Illustration 42
Implied contractual obligations 91
Independence of rights 47
Independent contractors 102, 123
Independent creation 32, 78, 108
Indirect translations 58, 69
Industrial espionage 87
Industrial secrets 86
Information 76–100
Infringement 43–45, 61, 62, 72
Injunctions 44
Inseparable contributions 30
Insolvency 127
Instructions 103–105
Intangibles 14
Intellectual creations 18, 19, 21, 29, 33, 45, 52
Intellectual property 7, 14, 48, 78, 79, 106, 107
Interdependent contributions 30
Interest 125
International courts 2, 3
International law 2, 3
Interpreters 12

Joint works 30, 31, 40, 63
Journalistic publications 27
Judicial procedures 11, 121
Jurisdiction 7–10, 128, 129
Jurisdiction clauses 9, 129
Jurisdiction conflicts 8

Know-how 77, 83, 85, 86, 91

Labour law 92, 93, 99
Labour law protection 101–113
Language 55, 56
Legal representatives 117
Legal systems 3, 4
Letters 116
Letters of intent 115
Libraries 43

Index

Licences 28, 32–35, 60, 72–74, 79, 108, 123
Limitations on copyright protection 40–43, 49, 70–72
Liquidated damages 125–126
Literary and artistic works 18
Literary works 22

Meaning 55
Mediation 129
Merit 20, 24
Minimum standards 2, 16, 47–49
Misappropriation 81–87, 97
Mistranslation 57
Moral rights 13, 33, 35, 59, 63, 67, 97, 109, 123
Most-favoured-nation 49
Musical works 22

National treatment 16, 47, 49
Neighbouring rights 14, 45, 46, 48, 49
News 25, 41, 71
Non-competition 105, 111, 112
Non-reciprocity 47
Notary public 116, 117

Offer 116
Official texts 41
Official translations 71
Original owner 67
Original works 21, 22, 54, 59
Originality 19, 20, 64
Ownership 28–30, 62

Paris Convention 14, 80
Partners 85
Partnerships 85
Payments 103–105, 109, 110, 113, 118, 120–122, 131
Penalty clauses 125–126
Performance agreements 34
Performance rights 36
Performing artists 45, 46
Personal data 90
Personal information 76, 78
Phonogram producers 45, 46
Political speeches 25
Power of attorney 117, 120
Pre-contractual agreements 89

Precedents 4, 5
Preliminary agreements 115
Privacy 89, 90
Private copies 42, 43
Private use 42, 60
Procedural rules 94, 128–130
Professional associations 11, 12, 121
Professional rules 10, 94
Professionals 86
Protected works 18–21
Provisional measures 44
Pseudonymous works 40
Public display rights 38
Public distribution rights 38
Public domain 69, 70, 83, 96
Public international law 2
Public lectures 41, 71
Public lending rights 38
Public policy 6, 7, 114
Public recitation rights 37
Publication 15, 118
Publication agreements 34, 114, 118, 119
Publishers' rights 119
Purpose of works 21

Quotations 41, 71

Registration 17, 27, 28, 34, 109, 117, 118
Regulations 10, 13
Remedies 43–45, 72
Remuneration 120–122
Rental rights 36
Reproduction right 35, 40, 61, 68
Reverse engineering 79
Revocation 73
Right of attribution 38, 59
Right of divulgation 39, 59, 97
Right of integrity 38, 59
Right of translation 58–62
Right to modify 39, 59
Right to withdraw from circulation 39
Roman law 3, 4
Rome Convention 14, 45

Scientific works 23
Secrets 77
Social security 104, 113

Software 23–26, 36, 39, 49–51, 75
Sole licences 34
Sources of the law 4
Specific performance 124
Speeches 25, 71
Stare decisis 4
Statutory law 4
Sublicences 74
Sweat of the brow 20

Taxes 113, 117, 122
Teaching 71
Term of protection 39, 40, 49, 70
Termination at will 127
Termination clauses 126–128
Termination notice 128
Termination of employment 105, 110
Theatrical works 22
Third parties 1, 131
Tort liability 92
Trade secrets 78, 82, 83, 86, 89, 91–93, 95–97, 100, 109–111
Trade unions 102, 104

Translation contracts 61, 73, 74, 114, 117, 118, 122
Translation rights 37, 67, 68
TRIPs Agreement 14, 16, 17, 25, 26, 36, 39, 43–50, 80, 82
Trust 91

Umbrella agreements 116
Undisclosed information 77
Unfair competition 80–86, 91, 120
Unforeseen circumstances 131
Universal Copyright Convention 48
Unjust enrichment 90, 91
Unwritten agreements 116, 130, 131

Wages 104, 120
Withholding taxes 122
World Trade Organization 48–50
Working hours 104, 113, 114, 120
Works made for hire 32, 33, 66, 67, 107–109, 123
Works of applied art 40
Written agreements 116

For Product Safety Concerns and Information please contact our EU representative GPSR@taylorandfrancis.com
Taylor & Francis Verlag GmbH, Kaufingerstraße 24, 80331 München, Germany

www.ingramcontent.com/pod-product-compliance
Lightning Source LLC
Chambersburg PA
CBHW070622300426
44113CB00010B/1624